Stacy Johnston
with
Boyd Hamlin and Cassey Holland

WISDOM OF HEROES
"If a T-Shirt Could Talk…"

Wisdom of Heroes
If a T-Shirt Could Talk...
Copyright © 2022 Stacy Johnston, Boyd Hamlin, and Cassey Holland

All rights reserved. No part of this publication may be reproduced, distributed or transmitted in any form or by any means, without prior written permission.

Published by
Dreamer Reign Media, LLC
P.O. Box 291354
Port Orange, FL 32129

www.dreamerreign.com

For Worldwide Distribution
Printed in the U.S.A.

ISBN: 9781952253232

Cover Design: C Marcel Wiggins

TABLE OF CONTENTS

Poem	5
Foreword	6
Chris Robinson – "I was made for this moment!"	9
Donnamarie Newkirk – "Next"	15
Harley Rhodes – "To give anything less than yourself is to sacrifice the gift."	23
Brigitte O'Michaels – "Everything is reciprocal"	29
Andy Hall – "Maximize your potential"	35
Darshan Shanti – "Love yourself first."	39
Joel Hawbaker – "All we have to do is decide what to do with the time given us."	43
Stephan Neff – "The past does NOT equal the future."	47
Justin Atherton – "Action kills anxiety"	55
Charles X – "Repent now for the Kingdom of Heaven is at hand."	61
Eva Fanari – "Your hands can be used for conflict or peace. Choose."	67
Mike D'Edgido – "Love for no reason."	73
Chris Luehr – "Be the hero. Live your best story."	81
Dr. Gloria Burgess – "Dream outside of the building!"	87
William Brown – "So go be you."	91
Drew Gerald – "Make truth the most important thing."	95
Chris DT Gordon – "Pass on perfection – go for greatness!"	101
Star Hansen – "Love your chaos."	107
Celia Kibler – "Laughter. It really is the best medicine."	113
Jake Doherty – "Keep your options open!"	121
Sapna Rad – "Do the work!"	125
Rayna Neisis – "It might be hard but It will be worth it!"	131
Kyle Spyrides – "Decide your destiny."	137
Nigel Harvey – " Fightin' on faith!"	145
MaryBess Johnson – "N.O.W. Not Over With"	151
Kurtis Cross – " Don't quit!"	157
Dwan Twyford – "The truth is in the red letters."	163
Sergio Gutierrez – "BOLD"	171
Koben Puckett – "There is no QUIT!"	175
Jess Bonasso – " Be the change you wish to see."	181

Vanessa Noemi – "You are your own medicine." 187
Phoebe Leona – "Move with joy!" 193
Jeannie Lynch – "Stop apologizing for your magnificence!" 197
Clair Bradshaw – "You have everything you need inside you" 201
Jamie Martin – "Be curiosity. Be courage. Be compassion." 205
Annette Maria – "There is no better time than Now!" 211
Mathilde Anglade – "You got this!" 217
Tana Inskeep – "Everything is 'figureoutable!'" 221
Hope Reger – "Invest in hope!" 227
Callie Knapp – "Be the role model!" 233
Ryan Rogers – "Be the light!" 237
Devin Tomiak – "Be empathetic." 245
Boyd Hamlin – "Act like you. You're the only one that can." 249
Richard Powell – "If you're not planning your life, someone else will." ... 255
Alex Pin – "If there are no roads, go make one!" 261
Tobey Geise – "You have all the answers within." 265
Olivia Cook – "Go be a bad-ass!" 269
Cassey Holland "Give yourself grace" 273
Paul Kennedy – "Travel. Now!" 277
Stacy Johnston – "Write the story. Dance the dance. Take the bow." 281
Next Steps 286
Authors' Bios 287
A Special Opportunity 291
Guardians Mission Statement 292
Rio Bravo Project 297
Acknowledgments 298

"I GOT THIS"
Poem by Darshan G. Shanti

I think big, act boldly, and demand astounding success
And I promise myself to never settle for anything less
I've got one life to live, so I give it all I've got
My time is now, and this is my shot

I absolutely can do whatever's in my heart
I simply make the decision, commit to it, and then start
Then I focus like a laser on the outcomes I desire
And I always go for more, constantly reaching higher

I dream bigger than the biggest dreams I've dreamt
And go for more than I thought I could attempt
In my success, I wholeheartedly believe
Since that's the surefire way that I'll always receive

I've got this, I'm a champion, so I stand proud
And I take a deep breath, then scream out loud
I am a winner and my success is up to me
And I will not stop until I reach my destiny

I'll spread my wings and begin to soar
And I'll go places I've never been before
I'll fly higher and higher, farther and faster
Cause it's my life and I am the master

FOREWORD

(phone randomly rings in the middle of the day)
Boyd: Hey Stacy, my friend, Christian Devries thinks we should turn the Hero Builder program that I created into a Podcast. Want to help me?
Stacy: How Fun!! I have no idea how, but let's do it!"
We took some time to look at all the podcast out there and asked 3 questions:

    1) What was missing in the world today and how could we use the concept of The Hero Builder program to make a positive impact?
    2) What would set us apart from the millions of podcasts out there?
    3) What information could we capture that would make a profound statement?

After some prayerful thought and many conversations, we came to the conclusion that there seemed to be a very skewed definition of Character and Integrity out there. All this technology and intelligence, but so much chatter about nothing. Where is all the wisdom hiding? Since the basis of the Hero Builder program is developing character and integrity in the youth by encouraging them to believe in and develop their own 'Inner Hero', what better way than to challenge the adults in our world to utilize the wisdom of Heroes and "Verb" the attributes? A "Show me don't tell me approach."

So, we did it. Jumped right in with both feet. Our quest was to discover how our guests defined the concept of Hero, who had inspired them along the way, and what would they say to encourage the world around them? We started The Hero Builder Podcast with friends of ours, people that we met at leadership conferences and individuals who are making a difference in the communities in which they lived. Our focus zeroed in on people that were doing everyday things in extraordinary ways. Soon, we found ourselves talking with heroes all around the world and discovered some things they all had in common – character, integrity, and grace. We were astounded at the responses we received on every podcast. Heroes were not in the movies, on stage at an event or doing big things in the world at large. Instead, they were people you would find in your own living room, across the street, in your school, church, community. The heroes that were mentioned could be found in your own backyard. After some time, Boyd stepped away to focus on the Hero Builder program. Cassey, who had been kind enough to guest co-host many times, agreed to step up take the co-host seat. Her insight and wisdom were a welcome addition.

One day we realized the statements people chose to share to encourage and empower others had to be put out there somehow. We looked at the shows we had recorded and realized we had asked over 200 people the same simple question," What does your T-Shirt say?" We had 200 completely different statements. Not one person repeated another. Two hundred statements of power, grace, encouragement, and hope. We started with this list of 50 as our first installment. Some of the statements are just a few sentences, some a few pages, but the power and grace offered speak to the heart and soul. There is information provided for each guest so you can connect to them or their program. There is also a section, 'Next Steps' that will show you how to turn the statements you read into virtual or live trainings for individuals, groups, businesses or communities, coaching options, and key note options.

Enjoy the Wisdom of Heroes!
Stacy, Cassey, & Boyd

Link to Un-Caped Heroes and Mid-Week Mind Candy
https://anchor.fm/un-capedheroes-thepodcast

*As of this publication, both the podcasts are alive and well under the direction of Stacy Johnston and Cassey Holland. We have rebranded from Hero Builder to Un-caped Heroes and Mid-week Mind Candy and it continues to be the most humbling and rewarding experience. To be a guest on our Podcast, reach out to us at: Herobuilder2020@gmail.com.

CHRIS ROBINSON

"I was made for this moment."

If a T-Shirt Could Talk...

About Me

Chris Robinson | EVP Entrepreneurial Solutions Group
MAXWELL LEADERSHIP

"It's not that you can't It's that you won't. The choice is yours"

maxwellleadership.com

Wisdom of Heroes

From Chris Robinson's Interview
(Episode #18)

STACY JOHNSTON: "If this was your day to make a t-shirt that stood out and said, 'this is Chris Robinson. This is my saying.' What's going to be on your t-shirt?"

CHRIS ROBINSON: "If I had to make a t-shirt today, the one line would be, 'I was built for this moment.' I was built for this moment. That's a phrase that I have used to carry me throughout the years. Public speaking, obviously, is one of the greatest fears on the planet. Sometimes as speakers, even after you've done it for a long time, to come to certain groups or titles of people that sometimes get you into opportunities where you feel like you're in over your head. I believe wholeheartedly that I'm in that situation more often than not. Here's what I learned from Mark Cole, President and CEO of John Maxwell Enterprise. We sat down at lunch one time and I said, 'What do you do when you're in over your head?' because we had recently just come back and we were inside the president of Guatemala's palace and I'm looking around the room like, how in the world did I end up here? How did I end up in a president's palace? This doesn't make sense. It doesn't register. And I said, 'Mark, you have to find yourself in that situation all the time. So what do you say?' He goes, 'Well Chris, I sit at the table, and I say this, 'I may be unqualified and I may be undeserving, but I'm fully confident that I belong at the table.' I said, 'Ahh! I love that!' I'm undeserving, I'm unqualified, but fully confident that I belong at the table. And so my mantra, as I get in over my head, or as there's any nerves that try to creep up on me. When I'm doing anything that may be beyond my scope and limiting belief begins to kick in; I simply repeat to myself, I was built for this moment. Because what you have to understand is that every single choice that you've made in life; every single choice that every single person in that room or in that boardroom or in that audience. Every single choice they've made has led to that very moment. Every single choice that you have made in life has led you to listening to this particular audio. And so I know that my voice is here to encourage and that there is no one else that is built for this moment, except for me. So, before I step on any major stage or before I step in any room I'm simply saying to myself, 'I was built for this moment.'"

Dear Reader:

You were built to overcome whatever is in front of you. You were built for this moment. No matter where you are in your life, no matter what challenges you may be facing, you are in the right place, at the right time. Someone out there is waiting for you to impact their life with your story. Don't make them wait any longer.

If a T-Shirt Could Talk...

DONNAMARIE NEWKIRK

"Next."

If a T-Shirt Could Talk...

About Me

God's loving daughter
Love is my favorite spiritual gift
My Why? Because God said so
Adopted
Adventurer
Always ready for The Next in life
Survivor of abusive relationships
Sagittarius
Mother
Furr-baby Mom of many
Advocate for Children in System
Google Queen
Gardener
Jazz, blues, spiritual music tickles my soul
Loves the ocean, sky, Ancestry, History, Antiques
Has a great ear, heart, soul for others....

Need to reachout a talk a spell. Call me. I love you

Cecile Donnamarie Newkirk
919-514-8881
Cdmwilder@yahoo.com

Wisdom of Heroes

From Donnamarie Newkirk's Interview
(Episode #22)

STACY JOHNSTON: "If there was a phrase that you would coin, this was your shining moment to pass on to the listeners today that golden thread of encouragement, hope, what would your t-shirt say today? What would you like to share with the listeners?"

DONNAMARIE NEWKIRK: "Thank you, Stacy, I would love to tell our audience that we are always preparing for the Next step, stage, periods in life, by completing the one we are in. So, my T-Shirt should say Next, as my life is surely a series of Nexts, some of which I know I tried my darnest to plan, some of which were plan B, and some that only God could of and did for my benefit. Either way, Next is absolute, a definitive process in our existence. We will all experience the Next whether job, family, society, in our personal lives and relationships, in all manner of our lives, there is the Next. We have some periods in life of which we can look back at past Next, and see what will be important to carry with us in the way of lessons. That is maturity and growth. There may be some past Next that we wish did not occur at all, but each Next is the moment in life that we need to focus upon, and the changes needed for us to grow. If we don't grow, we can't be happy. Lack of movement means stagnation, so when those moments of change with your Next happens, try not to be afraid of them. Draw upon all those past Next and realize that you have already been prepared to handle the future Next. If you think back to as far as elementary school, there were children we either played with or fought with, that at this moment in time, we wouldn't dream of having in our bubble. The why to that is because we have grown. Our Next had moved past the struggle of social norms and developing relationships and had become a catalyst for developing wisdom. Drawing on that, you can apply that same equation to all facets of life. Our dreams, relations, hopes, purposes all depend upon the Next level, stage, plan, change. You can do the pros and cons and analyze all you are able, but the most important is realizing that God has you, the universe loves you, and you have the ability to not fear the Next thing to reach all your goals. Enjoy the ride of Nexts in your life folks, there is so much waiting on you and you will be wonderful working on your purpose while you're waiting for your Next!"

Wisdom of Heroes

Dear Reader:

What does your Next look like?

We often say during a time of troubles, "What's Next?" Negatively, I suppose we are speaking new issues into existence, or positively, we are telling ourselves we are ready for the 'Next' stage, step or junction in life. Either way, 'Next' is an important word. It happens with or without our intervention or action, and it is for us to know how to appropriately use our 'Next.' Let's take a brief look on how important this unique four-letter word really is.

Life is not predicable. Sure, we plan, and then, sometimes life does a 360. We make choices, and we try with every part of our being to create the space in our minds to think through what our 'Next' steps may be in life. What job do I want, where to invest, to move, to eat, and the list of questions go on and on. Daily, weekly, monthly, yearly 'Next' are always a part of our cognitive functions, but what about the things that are not planned? That 'Next' is the part I am really wanting to focus on, because this is the 'Next' that can lead to stress, and difficulty in moving forward to a positive point in our lives.

The condition or state of not knowing what to do next applies to a lot of people, at any age and at different times in our lives. It can often lead to questions of "what am I doing with my life" or" what is my purpose" There are the things we try to squeeze our carcass into, to make money, buy respect, or earn fame. There are the truths that we steer away from, and the truth for our life that we cannot run from. The truth is, we can plan, but even the plan is guided by a higher authority, and for me, I have learned that God doesn't care about my comfortability or plans, because His agenda and script is already written. The Next, well that is written too, and time and maturity tells me that God's setups are designed set ups to achieve the Next that is coming.

However, this leads us to another topic, periods of growth come from the periods of not knowing or conditions in our life. Those set-ups

If a T-Shirt Could Talk...

from God, are there to offer elevation after devastation and for us to realize that alone, things can happen to me, and my Next with God, things happen for me. Whether pleasurable or painful, the Next will teach you and guide you toward your purpose. There is really no way around it, because it is not decided upon by you. It is however decided upon by our God. It is the Spiritual guidance to fulfill God's will over our lives that determines our Next. So how can we handle, or operate while Next is happening? Jesus told us in the book of John, "ye shall know the truth, and the truth shall make you free" So when the 'Next' is happening and you feel you are unsure at how to handle it, realize you are NOT in Control of the story.

I have had many periods of time that were difficult, stressful, and during those periods of time it took every ounce of my energy both mentally and physically, to make it through. What I've learned over time is all I could do was think about what I needed to do to get to the Next day. Notice I said mentally and physically, and you will know that early on, spiritually didn't enter my equation. But, with learning about my Next, I learned that what I wanted to do later in life does not equally equate to what I should be doing with my life. The biggest factor to our not wanting the Next to come, is fear. Fear, can put holes in our Destiny!! Fear in your life and trying to avoid the Next, will have you miss the major life moves that will help us to achieve that much planned, or orchestrated moment toward our purpose. We need to operate in our Next with faith, not fearful, and walk in the fact that God is faithful and His promises for an abundant life are true. Many people come as humble sweet children and grow to be mighty in the world, and leave a legacy written in books, some are the same child, but affect those in their local communities, all the while enjoying their plans or desires for a job, where to live, their families. Both are truly a testimony to not being fearful of our Next.

    A man known across the world was Martin Luther King, Jr. He was just a little boy, with many plans and desires as he matured. His life as a juvenile was testing, difficult, and poor in wealth. One of his many quotes is "Faith is taking the first step even when you don't see the whole staircase" I love that, but if I could ponder just a twist to that statement, make the word first, the word Next. Another way to say that would be speak it although you don't see it. That my friends is what our Next would look like. It is trust in the process, is trust in what God says over what we see. Remember we can't treat faith as a temporary location, because our Next is our destination. When our condition, or state or period in life is one of not knowing what to do Next, realize that the Next step toward your destination, your purpose, might include a staircase, a door, a move, so stop trying to figure it out. Please, just keep your eyes on God. He has given us great power and fear will hold your back, and is much less that the power you hold within, with faith. I think that human beings are either tangible, meaning we operate on the, what do we see, over what God wants us to be, in what we can't see. To have faith in the Next, we must be like God and value the spiritual over the physical here on earth. When we operate on what we have materially, like the Laodicean's in the books of Timothy and Colossians, we are materialistic, and the end result is we cannot have comfort in our Next, because we put more importance on what we have, over our spiritual selves. Another story in our Bible is that of Peter. He loved to fish. Even before our Lord was to be crucified, Peter was with the other Disciples, and he had been so much in charge, that they all waited for him to tell them what to do next. They were operating humanely world. So, Peter thought he would have them all go fishing and that way they would eat, and maybe even sell. However, their Next was not fruitful, because they were not faithful on God's word. Jesus had told them to wait for him, and so when all was found to be a failure and they returned to the shoreline, Jesus already had their meals caught and cooked. Their Next was a useless moment of energy that was not fruitful because they lacked the faith of their master Jesus. I operate the same on many moments, as we all do, because we are human. We live in another space in time, and on a spectrum of imperfection. So how do we just wait, in faith for our Next, and how do we know when that Next happens? I am not a professional here either, but one thing I do know is a lack of prayer to God is a lack of direction for us, and when my Next works much easily, it is one that is driven by God and not me.

In conclusion, I hope you now will see why I love the word Next. I want so much for you to understand that we cannot see the future without

If a T-Shirt Could Talk...

faith. We can enjoy the fruits of our desires with wealth and popularity and fame, but in order to have our purpose and be ready for the Next step, we mush be willing to have faith that this story is not ours. We can go to the store and buy our way to have anything we want. We can make decisions that are profitable and fulfilling, and yes, we should plan, but by asking God what to do with the 'Next', and be willing to hear what He says. We must trust the *promise* and the <u>promiser</u> that the 'Next' is not to be feared, no matter the difficulty and be ready to just go with the flow as our Next unfolds. We cannot see the blessing coming if we don't spend time with Him either, because just like a relationship here on earth, if you don't spend time with the ones you love, you won't be able to understand their will. My prayer for you as you learn to operate in the Next, is to know God will not always allow a now, but **He always will give you a NEXT!**...Be Blessed Yaw'll.

HARLEY RHODES

"To give anything less than yourself is to sacrifice the gift."

If a T-Shirt Could Talk...

About Me

Harley Rhodes is owner and creative designer at:
Dancing Cactus Designs
Address: 3621 NW 39th Expressway, Okc, Ok, 73112
Phone: 307-480-0301
Email: dancingcactusdesigns@gmail.com

Wisdom of Heroes

From Harley Rhodes' Interview
(Episode #24)

STACY JOHNSTON: "Let's pretend like this is your moment and you're going to caption the phrase. You're going to share a statement that you're going to pass on to our listeners today to bring out that hero in them to help them recognize that hero really exists within all of us if we just believe in it. What does your t-shirt say? What's your statement?"

HARLEY RHODES: "It's funny that you say you'd put it on a t-shirt because we've actually done this for several of our t-shirts, and I actually wear this on my back every day. I have it tattooed on my back. For those of you that don't know who I am, I was a very avid runner growing up and I have done long distance running for practically my entire life. I had a coach in high school, two coaches actually that used this quote. One was my very first cross country coach and the other one was my last cross country coach. They both told me this before my state finals run. It's a quote by Prefontaine. For those of you who don't know who Prefontane is, he was the first person to ever break four minutes in the mile. His big quote is, 'To give anything less than your best is to sacrifice the gift.' I take that really to heart. We're put on this earth to pursue all of these things that He has in store for us. And if you don't put forth your best effort, then it's a waste of those talents that you have been given. That's what I live by. I want to make sure that people see me and recognize me as a person that never gives up, and always tries to pursue everything with full heart. And that's where I lie, as far as business goes as well. I don't think that I would be where I am today, I don't think that I would be in the position that I am and the loyalty to what I have for my customers if I didn't give my 100% all, all the time. Now, I know it's hard to give that all the time, but as long as you recognize that when you're not giving it you're all- try harder. That's something that I think is going to be more important in this world and I think it's just going to make the world a little bit better. If you just continue to be the best person that you can really be."

STACY JOHNSTON: "I think that's a beautiful t-shirt. I would wear this shirt. Harley, I want to thank you so much for what you do and for being somebody's hero every single day. And one thing that we know is that we stand on the shoulders of those that have gone before us. And so, again, for myself and for the rest of our listeners, I'd like to thank you for being the shoulders that others can stand on to help find their hero, and recognize it's inside of all of us. So we hope they help you discover the hero within yourself in some way today. And until we meet again, let's go be somebody's hero."

Wisdom of Heroes

Dear Reader:

I'm Harley Rhodes and I want to help tell the world something about you. Like 100% of the people around you, your outer appearance is everyone's first impression of you. As vein as that may sound, it's a foundational truth. However, I believe it does not have to be a painful task or huge expense to just be you.

At Dancing Cactus Designs we started as makers of beautiful and affordable cowhide handbags. When I say "we" I really mean I. This company started in the living room of my one-bedroom rent house as I finished my senior year at Oklahoma State University in 2017. With a checking account balance of zero and my last pennies spent on a cheap sewing machine and a handful of cowhides I started making simple bags. Just like all the girl scouts do when selling cookies, I began targeting my friends and family to move and sell my newfound passion for bags. It worked, but of course at some point each of them had a bag for every day of the week and it was time to target a larger audience. Strangely enough, I saw this as an opportunity to use my degree in Sports Media Strategic Marketing to set the world in my sights and appeal to the masses. I quickly learned that I had so many tools at my disposal to make a direct connection with people through social media platforms. So with very little capital, but all the ambition in the world, I set out on a mission to make connections with customers one sale at a time.

Nearly four years later I find myself with that same explosive passion for people, but having grown my tribe to over 100 thousand followers on social media and enough of my handbags in the world to know I'm doing something right. Over time my design language has evolved and we've found such fun ways to take materials, which are available to everyone in the Western bag industry, to create such different and unique products from everyone else. When you run into another DCD bag out in the world, trust me you'll know it. As my customer base has grown many have reached out with stories of seeing another person with a DCD bag and striking up a conversation about it. Strangely enough, these encounters typically happen when folks are traveling or not in their normal surroundings. I love that my bags have often brought two complete strangers together in conversation to share their passion for this personal style statement. That's why I do what I do.

Proudly, I can now say "we" because of course by now I can't do this alone and I have a team of people helping to deliver this passion to our customers. Which brings us to now and how I want to be a part of your life. Everything we offer our customers serves a purpose, whether standing on their own or working together with other items in our collections. Their purpose is to help tell the world about your personality and who you are. I'd be proud and humbled to be in that journey with you.
Always,
Harley

BRIGITTE O'MICHAELS

"Everything is reciprocal"

About Me

Brigitte O'Michaels is a single mom to the 3 amazing children and has earn certificates in failures and successes in life. For over 20 years Brigitte has worked with organizations and individuals, helping them build their dreams, accelerate their results, to create richer, and more fulfilling lives that are in harmony with their Soul's purpose. She is the Founder of the DREAM BUILDER LAB private Facebook group where she shares Marketing, Money Mindset strategies to enable you live an expansive lif !

https://www.facebook.com/groups/marketingmoneymindsetmastery/?ref=share_group_link

As a highly sought-after speaker and trainer, Brigitte also finds pleasure in writing and has written 3 eBooks and also created an Experienced Product (Unstoppable Confidence RoadmapTM) where she shares the story and lessons of her life's journey from a toxic marriage .Brigitte also love helping women fix their crowns in her "Gurl Fix Your Crowns" Mentorship programs.

—

Brigitte O'Michaels
Speaker, Trainer, Coach, Consultant
brigittemichaels.com
johncmaxwellgroup.com/brigitteomichaels

Wisdom of Heroes

From Brigette O'Michaels' Interview
(Episode #33)

STACY JOHNSTON: "If you had a statement. If this was your moment to put Brigitte O'Michaels says on the front of that t-shirt. What would that statement be?"

BRIGITTE O'MICHAELS: "Everything is reciprocal . Everything. Whatever you sow that is what you get if you are an honest person, it will come back to you. That's what I would say. Be morally upright. Everything is reciprocal. The Bible talks of whatever we sow, we reap. And so that is what I leave with anyone who is listening to me today."

STACY JOHNSTON: "Thank you so much for sharing that. And for your inspiration, and for your integrity, Brigitte."

BRIGITTE O'MICHAELS: "Thank you."

BOYD HAMLIN: "This has been a great small conversation that we've had here and we can probably do this all day long. But because of the time frame that we are trying to do our podcast within, one of things I want to do is just shout out a special thank you to Bridgette, not only for being the hero to Stacy and now to myself, but also for sharing with us her hero, her mother. And we know that we stand on the shoulders of those who have gone before us. There's no doubt about that. But we thank you for being shoulders that we also can stand on today. And we hope that this has herofied you in a very big way today and until next time, I do want everyone to remember that there is a hero in everyone, and that does include you. But I want to leave you with the words of Brigitte's mother at the tail end of this podcast, and it's like this. *'Go to sleep, because tomorrow you will dream again.;'*

If a T-Shirt Could Talk...

Dear Reader:

How to silence the inner critic so you can truly focus on activities that produces results in your biz/life. Your life is waiting so get off that inner critic bus wagon..

She flung down on her sofa in dismay...No sale again this week she murmurs to herself. What am I going to do? She asked herself .Her heart beating fast! She is overwhelmed, confused and even angry with herself.. I am never good at anything she could hear that inner voice in her head and ears. Soon she couldn't stop the spiral of thoughts of precious experiences comes timeline down and she is afraid she is going to fail this one again!

Does this speaks to you in anyway or reminds of something..
- You're caught up in a cycle.
- You know the one.
- You've been talking down to yourself for a while.
- Every word in your mind points out your flaws and mistakes to where you think you're going to go crazy from listening to it if you haven't already.

You recognize the pattern right?.

Negative self-talk can be just this subtly harmful
- It gets in your head(courtesy of previous bad experiences, and negative input from people who don't always mean well.)
- It builds its home there It plays the same song on repeat, growing somehow worse with every retelling until you quit trying.
- Your dreams stall out, and you find yourself doing very little at all.

Well girlfriend it's Monday. Finally, you have another opportunity to take your life and business back and put an end to the negative self-talk once and for all so that you can achieve your desired money goals - I heard you whisper $10k months would feel soooo good. Easier said than done? Not necessarily. I gat you . I have some tools for you:

Wisdom of Heroes

Turn It Around

What is the positive counterpoint to this thought? For example, if you're worried about how bad you are with money, remind yourself of a time when you saved up for something you wanted, or think about a time when you invested in a great program and how good it felt afterward.

Create a Habit

If this negative thought is one which comes around often, what is the new thought you want to replace it with? How can you make this thought a habit? Consider this: the more you react in a new way to an old stimulus, the quicker a new habit is formed, and the old reaction disappears.

Change The Channel!

In the end, the only way to get rid of a negative thought is to consciously put a halt to it. Just A would change the channel with your remote control on a TV program that no longer serves you.

Rinse and Repeat these 3 steps and keep telling it to stop until it goes away completely. You don't have to listen to negativity but sometimes it becomes so firmly entrenched you might have trouble dislodging it by yourself. And if this is where you are, don't be afraid to ask for my help. Together let's lay this negative chatter to rest once and for all.

@CoachBrigitteMichaels

If a T-Shirt Could Talk...

ANDY HALL

"Maximize your potential."

About Me

Phone: +44 (0) 7743 841308
Email: andyhallcoaching@gmail.com
www.andyhallcoaching.com

Socail Media
facebook.com/andyhallcoaching
twitter.com/AndyHallCoach
www.linkedin.com/in/andyhall2710

"Until you make the unconscious conscious, it will direct your life and you will call it fate" - Carl Jung

Wisdom of Heroes

From Andy Hall's Interview
(Episode #43)

STACY JOHNSTON: If this is your chance to make a statement. That this is what Andy Hall believes and this is what I stand for and this is my statement. Andy, what does your t-shirt say?

ANDY HALL: "It would have to be 'Maximize your Potential.' That's one of those phrases that when I reflect on what maximizing your potential means, it does take me all the way back to my time with Alex. But, it really didn't resonate again with me until starting to work in the industry that we now are blessed to work in; and that's the personal development and personal growth industry. When I started to think about what is it that I would like to stand for as I started to develop my leadership and coaching business, it was really again to try and encourage people to have that belief in themselves. Just like a friend and a mentor of ours talks about holding your image, for me it's about maximizing your potential. It's about having that belief in your potential just like we were talking about a few months ago. That you can go on and do whatever it is you want to do. So, I'm always encouraging people to go maximize their potential."

If a T-Shirt Could Talk...

Dear Reader:

About Andy Hall Coaching

Andy Hall Coaching specializes in leadership development, customer service and people-based organizational transformation & behavioral change. Andy is a qualified ICF ACC Certified Executive Business Coach as well as a Business NLP Practitioner.

Privacy Policy

Contact Andy
+44 (0)7743 841308

andy@andyhallcoaching.com
Minety, Wiltshire

DARSHAN SHANTI

"Love yourself first."

About Me

    Darshan is the founder and President of Freedom Incorporated, Inc. He is transformational speaker and a published author of 2 personal development books, 2,000 inspirational poems, and 2 children's books. Over the past 2 decades, he has given 500 talks that have inspired over 30,000 people to believe in themselves and live their truth so they can reach their fullest potential.

Direct/Text: 505-340-9878
darshan@darshanshanti.com
www.darshanshanti.com

From Darshan Shanti's Interview
(Episode #60)

STACY JOHNSON: I'm in, I got it. I like that motivation. Make me want to get up in the morning, and go for it and excel. So just thank you for that encouragement in your voice. So Darshan, if this was your minute and you had an opportunity to make a statement to the whole world, what would your t-shirt say?

DARSHAN SHANTI: Love yourself first. Period. If you don't love yourself, it's all for nothing. It's like when you're on the plane, and the oxygen mask drops down. You have to put it on yourself first, then your kid, because if you pass out no one is going to take care of your kid. You have to love yourself, fully, unconditionally, first.

Closing Statement: "I'm very, very grateful too. This is one of the best interviews I've ever had, you two are a credit. God Bless You, and thank you for doing what you're doing, and helping people to not only share what their vision is of being a hero, but then when you put it out in this format, and now all these other people are going to hear it. They're going to hear it, and it's going to bring out the hero in them."

If a T-Shirt Could Talk...

Dear Reader:

One of the greatest "secrets" in life is to love yourself first! You are the most beautiful creation in the entire YOUniverse. You were created out of love and love is the energy of creation. You are love. You can be nothing else. You must own that.

So forget about your past. It doesn't matter what anyone else thinks about you. All that matters is what you think, feel, and believe about you. The truth is that you are priceless, an immeasurable treasure. Your value is so immense, there is no measure. In fact, the moment you take full responsibility for your greatness, your magnificence, your pricelessness, and love yourself unconditionally, then live that way without exception, that's when you will end all of your internal struggles and once and for all, have the life you've always wanted.

The question is, how do you go about doing that? Well, start talking to yourself in the most positive way you can. And do it all day, every day. When you first arise, even before you open your eyes, say something like, "Every day in every way I'm getting better and better." But don't just say the words, FEEL THEM. It's the feeling that is the key to help you change your life most quickly. Think it. Feel it. Believe it. Know it. Be it. Live it. When you do that, things will change and the floodgates of prosperity will open up. Prosperity is much more than just money. It's love, it's joy, it's fulfillment, it's fun, and whatever else that is important to you.
And here is a poem I wrote that I say to myself first thing. It uplifts and inspires me. It motivates me to make the best of my day. And it keeps me focused on what I want and where I'm going. Feel free to use it or come up with a positive phrase, sentence, or paragraph that speaks to your heart and feeds your soul. Whatever you have to do to love yourself first, do it! There's nothing more important!

JOEL HAWBAKER

"All they have to do is decide what to do with the time we are given."

About Me

Joel is a blended family coach, an award-winning teacher, author, speaker, and host of '10CBF: A Podcast for Blended Families.' He loves helping blended/stepfamilies overcome obstacles and grow by teaching them the 10 Commandments for Blended Families. Joel is a divorced and remarried father of two. He currently lives in Alabama with his wife and their two rescue dogs Bruiser and Butterscotch.

His first book, Inverted Leadership: Lead Others Better By Forgetting About Yourself was a #1 best-seller on Amazon. He is currently at work on a book about blended families as well as a 31-day devotional for blended families. Having studied and played soccer at both Covenant College (Georgia, USA) and Oxford University (England, UK), Joel has a B.A. in History and a passion for literature as well as a love for sports, and he looks forward to taking a dream vacation of visiting Hobbiton in the Shire.

From Joel Hawbaker's Interview
(Episode #64)

STACY JOHNSTON: "Okay, without further ado, Joel. We've heard the most incredible things from you. We've heard words that are missing in our world right now in so many ways. We've heard grace, we've heard humility, we've heard honor, respect, courage, never stop, adaptability. I mean, those are strong words and what a wonderful attribute that you have to own those words and have the life to have been exposed to them. So, if this is your chance, and you're going to make a statement to the world. What does your t-shirt say?"

JOEL HAWBAKER: "Well, it's going to have a quote on it from one of my all time favorite authors and one of my all time favorite books, and that is JRR Tolkien's 'The Lord of the Rings.' And there's a quote in that book where the character Gandalf says to another character, 'All we have to decide is what to do with the time that is given to us.' Because I firmly believe that we all get 24 hours in a day, we get however much time God puts us here on Earth, and really the only decision we have to make is; how are we going to spend our time? Are we going to spend it loving other people? Are we going to spend it serving other people? Are we going to spend it helping other people? Or, are we going to spend it just pursuing things that really don't have any eternal value? And so I think that's what my t-shirt would say, "All we have to decide is what to do with the time that was given to us."

STACY JOHNSTON: "That is beautiful. And, you know what you're exactly right. All we can do is make the next right choice and own the minutes that we're standing in. I want to thank you so much for the time that you spent with us today. For giving us your story, for sharing your hero with us, and your journey. This information will be so valuable. The connection to a group such as this will be valuable to so many people. So, I don't know about you, Boyd, if you've got anything else to add, but I can't think of a more appropriate way to end today's show than to end with Joel's quote. 'All we ever have to decide is what to do with the time that is given us.'"

If a T-Shirt Could Talk...

Dear Reader:

Make the decision!

STEPHAN NEFF

"Love yourself first."

If a T-Shirt Could Talk...

About Me

Dr Stephan Neff is passionate about demystifying mental health problems and helping the people around him live a life so full of joy that yesterday is jealous of today. Born in Germany, Stephan has studied medicine at the prestigious Heidelberg University before travelling and working around the globe. Nowadays he has settled down as an anaesthetist in beautiful New Zealand and has become a bestselling author and advocate for mental health and addiction.

He is uniquely qualified in this role. After all, a lifetime of trauma led Stephan to drown his sorrows, only to find that the critters can swim. As an alcoholic in recovery, he has experienced addiction and mental health problems first-hand. After successful rehabilitation, Stephan is now an expert in living a life so fantastic, that alcohol has simply no role to play. He shares this passion through his podcast, YouTube channel, and other social media (all titled "My Steps to Sobriety").

In his book "My steps to Sobriety" he shares the lessons he has learned as a doctor and as a man. And the truth is simple - The past does not equal the future. Every alcoholic can turn his life around, one little decision at a time. This book shows how to do it.

Wisdom of Heroes

From Stephan Neff's Interview
(Episode #78)

STACY JOHNSTON: "With your knowledge, with your path you have walked, and where you are today. If this was your moment to make a statement to the world, what would your t-shirt say?"

STEPHAN NEFF: "It would actually be a very big t-shirt in all fairness, probably sort of a 12XL to get everything on there, but it would be somewhere along the lines of, 'The past does not equal the future.' the past does not equal the future. You can do it, and you are not alone."

STACY JOHNSTON: "Stephan…I know that we are working with your time being in New Zealand and you've been so kind to give us your time and I do not want to take unfair advantage of that. So there's two things. Could you please let our audience know how they can reach you if they would like to connect to you in your program, and would you give us a closing statement?"

STEPHAN NEFF: "Absolutely, for you out there, do not give up! There is a good reason that you're listening to this, because there's trauma and heavy heart in your chest. Do not give up. You are not alone. You might feel helpless and hopeless now, but please, please, please reach out. Find your tribe. Find those people who are like you, that have gone through similar trauma and learn from them, what they did to get better, because there is that beautiful life waiting for you. You just probably can't see it right now. And if you guys want to know more about me, you can go to my website which is www.mystepstosobriety.com I'm quite active on Instagram and all social media apart from Twitter and all my handles are My Steps to Sobriety. So, look me up. I've written a book about my experiences, again, the book title is My Steps to Sobriety and it's out there in ebook, normal format. So guys, there is help out there, and if you don't know where to start, you could do far worse than actually start with my book, because I'm laying out my story and I'm also laying out action plans and all the tips and tricks that Ive learned in the seven years now of successful recovery."

If a T-Shirt Could Talk...

Dear Reader:

"God, grant me the serenity,
To accept the things, I cannot change;
Courage to change things I can
And wisdom to know the difference."

The words penetrated me like a laser beam. How could they possibly know how I feel? I had only just arrived here, yet, the words spelled out the existential question hidden deep in my tormented soul. The first time I ever read them was my first day in rehab.

I was literally the proverbial deer caught in the headlights. As an anaesthetist I was a specialist in my field. Type A personality, perfectionist, idealist, empathic, a heart the size of my home town - the works. But deep inside I was a broken man. The evil twins of shame and guilt were constant companions. And they had a knack of replaying "The Best of Stephan" at 3.30 am: everything I could have possibly done wrong over the last 40 years. But guilt and shame paled into insignificance when it came to resentment and anger. Oh boy, now we were talking. After all, I had gone through some hard times. I had stood up to the powers in charge to defend the patients in my care. I was the fighter, the knight in shining armour who was rescuing the damsels in distress. Well, I guess at the end I was more like Don Quixote fighting wind mills. But I guess that is a side effect of a litre of vodka a day (and then some).
"Hi, I am Thomas, I am an addict."
"Hi, I am Beatrice, I am an alcoholic."
Suddenly - silence. Looking up, it was my turn to introduce myself to 20 complete strangers. Where was the hole to hide in?
"Hi, I am Stephan. I am an alcoholic."

Boom. There it was. I only said the words in order to fit in. After all, surely, I wasn't an alcoholic! I am a doctor. Ok, yes, there have been huge psychosocial stressors and more pain and trauma than I cared to remember. Surely, it was absolutely normal to have a drink or ten to numb the pain?

Wisdom of Heroes

In that moment, something changed in me. It was as if the dam started to break. Speaking out those few words changed me forever. Hearing those words out of my own mouth caused a flood of emotions that made the world's scariest roller coaster look like a baby swing. Shame, guilt, elation, freedom, embarrassment, joy, surprise - hell, how many emotions can you possibly feel in 10 seconds? I don't remember too much of the following hour. I was too engrossed in the emotions that were washing over me. Emotions… those pesky little things I had tried to drown for the last 20 years. And here I was, suffering the onslaught without a crutch to lean on. No music to play, no film to watch, no bottle of wine to alter my state. Simply me and my emotions.

Could my story have ended up in a different way? Yes, I guess, prison or death are the common alternatives for addicts. Simply spoken, I had come to the point where even my marinated brain recognized that I had to change. That I could not continue as before. That the old me had to die and that I had to reinvent myself. But how? My rehab was based upon the 12 steps of Alcoholics Anonymous. In a nutshell:
- The first three steps show you how to give up.
- Four, five and six teach you how to own up.
- Seven, eight and nine reveal how you make up.
- Ten, eleven and twelve make you grow up.

It sounds easy, doesn't it? Reality is, each and every step is as painful as peeing glass shards. Rehab at times feels like that. But as with every training, things get easier. Especially if you have a team that shows you what to do. In my case, I had to relearn the basic fundamentals that had been missing for so long in my life - honesty, transparency, authenticity and integrity.

Rehab is where the magic happens. Once you have detoxed you are ready to adopt new habits. You quickly learn that you are either working on your recovery or working on your relapse. 80% of alcoholics relapse in their first year of sobriety. Alcohol is a mighty foe who must not be underestimated!

If a T-Shirt Could Talk...

Could you get clean all by yourself? In my opinion, this is simply impossible. Even the best book or the best course cannot replace a skilled person listening to you and reflecting what you are saying (or not saying for that matter). After all, you can't bullshit a bullshitter. In my rehab, I had to realize that every person treating me (bar a few of the doctors) was actually an addict. The yoga-instructor who in the past turned up drunk to her clients was now leading a class for the inmates. The counsellor who runs the dreaded 10 am "emotions "-meeting had been sitting in my chair a few years back. The smirk on my case-manager's face said it all - she had been in my shoes in the past. Her brain had fought tooth and nail to hold onto the old destructive coping mechanisms just as much as mine did right now.

But there was one big difference between "us" and "them." Our guardian angels were well-groomed, relaxed in their confidence and displayed an aura that was palpable. They clearly had their ducks in a row. Me, I at best had squirrels that were hosting a rave.

So, with the right guidance in due course I was able to address resentment, anger, depression, anxiety and PTSD as the root causes for my attempts to escape reality. Recovery is like an onion. Rehab strips back one layer at a time to reveal all the trauma and negative emotions you tried to hide so cleverly behind a myriad of masks. I learned to focus on one problem, and make a start. Rehab gave me the push that I needed. Once you rip off the first band-aid life will never be the same again. But I assure you, this is no walk in the park. Expect a bumpy ride! The moment you have dealt with one trauma you find two other things that have held you back. You have barely opened one wound when you realize how much that pus has influenced other parts of your life. This journey is painful and difficult. Because of that, there is no person walking this Earth who shows more courage, honesty, dignity and integrity than an addict in recovery. Change doesn't happen overnight. It doesn't happen in one session. There is not one magic meeting. For me, the pus had drenched my whole body and soul. Sometimes the stink was obvious, sometimes it was cleverly hidden by mental constructs I had created to deal with emotional trauma. There was so much pus hidden in my body and it needed to be drained, one pustule after the other. That was a hard pill to swallow for me at the time but by now I had learned to trust the people I had paid to make me better.

Recovery is like starting a big jigsaw puzzle where you never know how many pieces there are. And guess what, there is no picture to guide you. So, you keep working on the puzzle, one piece at a time. You address a problem until you are content that you have either sorted it or that you truly cannot do anything more about it. One way or the other, you are ready to move on to the next puzzle piece.

And the journey never stops. Only because you got the monkey off your back does not mean that the circus has left town. Unless you address the reasons for your drinking you will not succeed in changing your behaviour. Instead, you simply change the poison. And there is so much to choose from: sugar, porn, smoking, other drugs, gambling, work, extreme sports and sex are just waiting to take the role of the alcohol.
The temptations will always be there. I am an addict after all. But I have learned to look after myself. I have found the triggers that make me want to self-destruct. HALT is all I need to go off the rails. When I am hungry, angry, lonely and tired - oh boy! Give me three out of those four triggers, and even today I get thoughts about alcohol and sugar. Give me four of these triggers at the same time and I can guarantee you that my addiction wants to come out to play.

However, I do no longer feel guilty and shame-ridden when my brain suggests a drink. I rather see it as a message that I have slipped in looking after myself. In the same way I have learned to surf waves of anxiety and deal with deep dark mood holes. From now and then, I throw a pity-party but I do no longer pitch a tent over there. When people remind me of my past, I remind them that I don't live there anymore. What was once my mess is now my message. The old phoenix had to burn for the new Phoenix to rise from the Ashes. And instead of being ashamed about

How to Contact Me

it I nowadays host the YouTube show and podcast "STEPS TO SOBRIETY" to demystify addiction and mental health problems. I am still an addict. But nowadays I am addicted to life. I truly love the new me!

1. https://www.youtube.com/channel/UCQ5Rgw59jOX4y3iDeMAXpwQ (YouTube show)
2. https://stephanneff.podbean.com/ (podcast)
3. https://www.facebook.com/stepstosobriety
4. https://www.instagram.com/stepstosobriety/
5. https://www.linkedin.com/in/stephan-neff-author/
6. https://www.mystepstosobriety.com

JUSTIN ATHERTON

"Action kills anxiety."

If a T-Shirt Could Talk...

About Me

In dealing with countless high stress and volatile situations Justin Atherton learned that integrity—in every aspect—is the most important factor in whether someone succeeds or fails. With over 16 years of Law Enforcement experience in SWAT, Investigations, Training and Leadership roles, Justin develops and shares tactics and techniques that help forge the next generation of leaders. After departing the SWAT team, he launched *Confidence Unchained*, a company that teaches these same leadership principles to those from any walk of life. From business owners, CEO's and entrepreneurs, Justin has helped people across a broad range of industries build their own Peak Performance and regain their EDGE. Detailing the mind-set and principles that enable Detectives and SWAT teams to accomplish the most difficult missions, *Confidence Unchained* shows how to apply them to any person, family or organization. The three pillars of the program focus on a specific topic such as Mental Toughness, Emotional Fortitude and Health Awareness, explaining what they are, why they are important, and how to implement them in any environment. Powerful coaching and direct application, *Confidence Unchained* revolutionizes personal consulting and challenges those everywhere to fulfill their ultimate purpose and keep their EDGE.

Email: Justin.Atherton@ConfidenceUnchained.com
ConfidenceUnchained.com

From Justin Atherton's Interview
(Episode #82)

STACY JOHNSTON: "So with all the things we've talked about today and the people that you've discussed and the emotions that you've been through and the things that you teach other people. If this was your moment to make a statement, what would your T-shirt say?"

JUSTIN ATHERTON: "You know, there's a few things but I would say one of the things that really stands out is 'Action kills anxiety.' Because we tend to sit in this space right before we do something or if we are contemplating adventure or making a phone call, or starting a business, those moments of anxiety. But when you're in the action; when you are doing it, it's not there anymore. I can equate it to, you know, riding in the back of a SWAT truck getting ready to go, you know, assault a house, and there's a level of anxiety there before you get there. You're thinking about everything that could go wrong, all the different possibilities. But once you jump off that truck, there's no more anxiety. Once you're in the moment, anxiety is gone. So rather than sitting there in that anxious state, take some action."

STACY JOHNSTON: "That my friend is very sound advice. I think we spend a lot of time anxious about the outcome of work. Could we be and so many times it prevents us from moving forward at all. We let the anxiety be bigger, and what a waste. What a beautiful message. I think that's a great message. So, let me ask you this; if you were going to send a message, if you have something to say, and you wanted to close out with that message. Let me take a moment, let me give you the stage, and how about you close it out today with what you would like to say to our audience."

JUSTIN ATHERTON: "I appreciate the opportunity to close out the show with your audience. You know, Stacy and Boyd, I would say that we need to take time to think about what's bothering us. What is going on in our heads? Going back to the idea of the gap between reacting and responding, nothing is a big deal unless it's some type of emergency situation where someone's life is on the line and hopefully no one's put in that type of situation. But besides that, nothing is really that big of a deal to get upset about, to take out your pain and frustration on someone else. So give yourself those moments to just think about how you want to react and how you want to respond and just take that moment to think. What are the reactions here? What is going to be created from this? So just take those little moments to really think about and choose your actions purposefully."

Dear Reader:

For those of you currently lacking confidence in one or more aspects of your life, I want you to understand this: Confidence is not something you are either born with or not. It's not even a skillset that you can work on or obtain. Confidence is a state of being. Once you are able to be comfortable in your own skin and create your values and beliefs, then you can unchain that confidence hiding inside of you. My name is Justin Atherton, the founder of Confidence Unchained. Are you ready to step into your confidence? Reach out at ConfidenceUnchained.com or Justin.Atherton@ConfidenceUnchained.com.

Justin W Atherton
Peak Performance Consultant
ConfidenceUnchained.com

If a T-Shirt Could Talk...

CHARLES X

"Repent now for the Kingdom of Heaven is at hand."

About Me

Charlesex83@gmail.com
Instagram, You Tube, Apple I-Tunes, Amazon, FB, Charles X.

Insta
@charlesxmusic

FB
CharlesXOfficial

From Charles X's Interview
(Episode #85)

BOYD HAMLIN: "There is a lot of stuff that we could pack into this conversation, but I would like to know. What would you pass on? And what would you like to pass on to others that impacted you? And you can go from your hero into this. What do you really want to say to those who listen to you and who come alongside you in your sphere of influence?"

CHARLES X: "I would say don't follow my example, obviously, but follow the example I follow. Follow the example of Christ because even what you just said recently, or what you just said right now, which is how you have to deny yourself pretty much in how you can't have Jesus and your own way. And so right now with the way that the world is going, even with this last album that I'm telling you I'm making, and with the tumultuous times that we're in; I'm one sometimes my soul wonders. I want to set the record clean with this last album as far as Charles X and I just don't want to lose my gift of heaven and my grace from Jesus Christ. I sometimes feel like I'm playing a dangerous game because I'm trying to reach the world. And He says, 'be in the world but not of it.' So I'm trying to reach the world and because I see how sad everybody is, and I see all these problems, and if I can leave them with something it's, 'The reason the world is falling is because they have fallen away from God.' And that is so true, because even with me and trying to reach these people one time, I wonder, am I still going on my will or does God want me to help these people? Does He want me to say this last thing because, you know, sometimes as Christians, we want to go into our little Christian bubble. We only want to talk to Christians and we only want to do that and for some reason I feel like He wants me to speak one more time to the world. He said, I did not come to condemn the world, that the world should be saved through Me, right? So I feel like if there's one thing that I can really tell the world, it's don't follow my example. Don't follow your example. Don't always go with your heart because that's not true either—the heart is wicked. So if there's one thing you could do, sit down, read that Bible, pray every day and ask the Holy Spirit and ask the Lord to tell you what am I supposed to do here? And usually that's the scariest thing to do. I'm doing sold out shows in Paris. I'm out doing all kinds of press and all of this stuff you get, the more you realize that none of this stuff is real. These are material things that are going to fade away. My saying also that I would love on the shirt would be 'repent now for the kingdom of heaven is at hand.' You can feel that, and if you can't feel that then that means that you might be in a very dark place, and I wouldn't want to be in that place. Repent now, for the kingdom of heaven is at hand. BOYD HAMLIN: I'm not going to say anything else to that because I think that was said very, very well. And I'm just going to leave it right there where it is. And if you haven't heard that message, listeners, go back, rewind this thing and listen to it again and again, until you get that message that he just gave us."

CHARLES X: "Or read your Bibles, because Jesus Christ said it way before me. I believe that I'm confessing with my mouth and believe in my heart Jesus Christ is Lord. That's all."

BOYD HAMLIN: "Absolutely. Absolutely."

Wisdom of Heroes

Dear Reader:

I am D.D aka Charles X

Reflecting on my interview with Hero Builder has made me realize how easy it is to say something and how hard it is to follow. Since that interview, life has changed so much for me and the whole world. Covid stopped us in our tracks, the world is becoming more confused and the children are being attacked in every way. For the first time I am understanding why adults used to look into the air of nostalgia and tell me how much things have changed since they were young with a melancholy tone in their voice and fragments of wonder in their eyes. I think a small part of that is them seeing how much things have changed and a bigger part of it being them realizing how much and how little they had to do with it.. By that, I guess I mean that most people, when they are young, see the world through rose colored glasses. To them the world is seemingly progressing as the old ways start to move out and the "new" and "cool" ways start moving in.

Then you hit an age where you suddenly realized these "new" and "cool" things were never new or cool at all. More importantly, if you look at the root of these things, they were always there to separate you from God and the morals your parents taught you, that their parents taught them. The trick is that by the time you learn all of this, it's too late and a new generation has already come along and started their interpretation of "New" and "cool" and even if you try to tell them you've been down that path and where it will lead, they'll just call you old as they continue to do it because it's not yet their time in the cycle of life to understand. The one thing that hasn't changed is the fact that the world still needs the Most High God and probably more than ever now. With the times being so tumultuous and unsure, just remember that this is what was predicted to happen long ago.

Even more than the struggles happening in the world, I find myself struggling with myself a lot. Every day I get older and everyday I become more aware of my self and the world. All of our flaws and ego driven

If a T-Shirt Could Talk...

decisions that separate us from a holy God. I am starting to realize this is the reason why our Lord and savior Jesus Christ died on the cross. As flawed as I am, I am thankful that He loves me so much to die for my sins so that His righteousness will be counted when it's time for judgement and not my own shortcomings. It's very humbling.. It makes me think of this saying I heard recently that goes, "My heart aches but I have joy." And I thank the Lord for that. The message still remains the same, "Repent now, for the kingdom of heaven is at hand." There is only one true Hero in my opinion and He died on the cross and rose 3 days later, conquering death and saving us all. His family, friends and neighbors all watched Him dying on that cross as a murderer and thief was set free. We know this to be true and are still self centered and self righteous at time... OH Lord please save us. Please give me and whoever is reading this the courage to spread your good news around this Earth and to stay the salt of the world. Hard times are coming, give us your joy and your rest. Let us lean on your strength and not on our own understanding. Let us remember this is not our home. Most importantly forgive me Father... I pray you will finish your work with me and that I can be found acceptable in your sight. Free me from this sin in Jesus name I pray. Amen.

EVA FANARI

"Your hands can be used for conflict or peace. Choose."

If a T-Shirt Could Talk...

About Me

Contact Information:
Cellphone: 505-506-0097
Office phone: 505-828-1000

From Eva Fanari's Interview
(Episode #93)

STACY JOHNSTON: "Let's take all this gold that you've laid on us. Let's take all this knowledge and all this self awareness and all these beautiful things that you've shared with us in this conversation. Thank you, by the way for your candor and your transparency in it a'll. With all of that in mind, if this was your chance, Eva, and you had an opportunity to make a statement to the world, what would your t-shirt say?"

EVA FANARI: "I think my t-shirt would say what I just said a little bit earlier, it would say, 'Your words are the tools for conflict and for peace. Choose.' I think the world needs this statement right now and I think every time I look in the mirror it's a great statement or a reminder for me too."

STACY JOHNSTON: "I think that's beautiful. Use your words as a tool for conflict or for peace. Choose well. Nice, beautiful Eva. That's beautiful. I have had more fun and I feel like I have been blessed is a better way to say it. I mean fun is a good word, but blessed is a better way to say it. What has happened in my world is I have these interviews and I get to talk to people like yourself that just do extraordinary things in the lives of other people by the way you live your life and the light that you shine. To get to hear your quotes and your stories and your statements to the world is a gift, so thank you very much for opening that gift for us today."

EVA FANARI: "Thank you so much for having me, and I absolutely love your little podcast, I have to tell you. I have been listening to it more intensely over the last week; just to prepare. I listen to a lot of episodes and I've listened to it in the past as well, and I think it's just wonderful to hear from people who come across as ordinary people and realize that they are actually extraordinary. Everybody else who we think is extraordinary is ordinary. Does that make sense?"

STACY JOHNSTON: "It makes perfect sense."

BOYD HAMLIN: "Oh yeah, that does make sense. Good!"

If a T-Shirt Could Talk...

EVA FANARI: "It's a gift you are giving to the world, and I'm so happy that you invited me to be a part of it."

STACY JOHNSTON: "We're honored that you chose to be with us today."

EVA FANARI: "Thank you!"

BOYD HAMLIN: "Yes Eva, just in closing I think what Stacy and I would really like for you to do for us and for our listeners is just to end just one final time with the phrase that you have put on your t-shirt so that it speaks not just for today but it speaks for our days to come. Just close us out real nicely with your phrase one more time so that our listeners can get that point if they lost it somewhere in the rest of our conversation."

STACY JOHNSTON: "Ok, 'your words are the tools for conflict and for peace. Choose well.'"

Wisdom of Heroes

Dear Reader:

The Magic of Words

An old adage says, "speaking is silver, silence is gold." It basically says to stop talking. Why is one of the oldest wisdoms so final about our words? Recently, I had a meeting with a client to discuss the value of her investment property. We were sitting in an outdoor café, sipping tea and catching up. She was impressed by how much her property had gained in value in just two years, she was grateful to have her health, and she was happy to be in such a lovely cafe. In the middle of all that happiness, her phone rang. She glanced at the caller ID, and said "Let me take this. It'll be just a few minutes." If you don't count "mhmm..."and the final "Can I call you back later?" as talking, she did all the listening. I didn't hear the conversation but I could see the conversation in her body. Her shoulders slumped forward, her jaw tightened, and her smiling lips transformed into a thin horizontal strip.

When the call was over, she now noticed the cafe patio was really cold and dirty, she mentioned she needed to lose weight, and she thought her property could have performed much better. I had to ask, "What was the call about?""Oh, nothing urgent. Someone I know is having problems and wanted to vent. I can talk to her later." Even though my client smiled again by the time we parted, she hadn't made a full recovery. Studies show that stressful state from negative news and interactions stays in our bodies for hours and even days. The heightened levels of stress hormones remain in the blood stream and the organism is in a survival mode. All of this because of words. In Japanese, the term Kotodama ("word spirit") is the idea that words have magical power to alter physical reality. The most famous Aramaic word is, arguably, abracadabra. What comes in mind when you think of it? A magician? It's literally a magic word! You almost expect me to pull a rabbit out of a hat. Something has to materialize from nothing. The original meaning of this word is it will be created in my words; something always materializes from a word. Even though we may not have a specific term for magical quality of words in our language, we know the meaning of it. Words, once released, lay like a blanket over the

If a T-Shirt Could Talk…

receiver. Some words are light and uplifting, others are heavy. The former lift people up like Aladdin's magic carpet. The latter weigh them down like tarp and block the light altogether. Regardless of their weight, our words carry a tremendous influence. The words you choose to say, in which order you arrange them, and how you say them come with an energetic load.

Do you lift the people around you? Or do you sink the people around you? Not only is complaining abuse of the other person's energy but when you release your heavy words upon another person, forget not that the blanket of your words has a signature on it – yours. That signature will hold on to you. As an anchor, it'll keep youattached to the carpet and keep you stuck to the bottom. While the other person can walk away eventually, you are stuck with your creation. But guess what? The same applies for praise and encouragement. Once created by you, your signature is like a string attached to the uplifting energy of your kind and positive words. It boosts everyone's well-being. Do you remember Dumbledore's words to Harry? "Words are, in my not so humble opinion, our most inexhaustible source of magic, capable of both inflicting injury and remedying it."

J. K. Rowling, Harry Potter and the Deathly Hallows An old adage says, "speaking is silver, silence is gold." That is, if you're not mindful of your words. Thus, I would like to take the liberty of modifying the old adage as follows: Speaking is silver, silence is gold, and speaking with kindness is pure diamonds.

You can find Eva at evafanari.com

MIKE D'EDGIDO

"Love for no reason."

If a T-Shirt Could Talk...

About Me

Mike D'Egidio
Associate Broker Realtor
Realty One of New Mexico
7441 Alambeda Blvd NE Suite B.
Albuquerque, NM 87109

Email: Mike@abqhousebuying.com
Cellphone: 505-414-4042
Office phone: 505-883-9400

From Mike D'Egidio's Interview
(Episode #96)

STACY JOHNSTON: "Mike, when you look at all this gold that you've laid on us today. It's evidence that you were taught and raised in a servant's mindset and a servant's heart, and you've continued on that path. So, if this was your golden opportunity and you had a chance to stand before the world and make a statement, what would your t-shirt say?"

MIKE D'EGIDIO: "I've just got a quick tangent or aside before I tell you what my t-shirt would say. In a world today, where it seems that the magnifying glass; whether it's social media, mainstream media, whatever other red herrings everybody's kind of concentrating on and looking at. Whatever filter you're looking at through life and stepping back and saying, there is so much hatred that's self portrayed, that's objectified to other people, that it's so easy to be trapped in the negative. And in the mindset of just like, well, nothing ever happens. You know, nothing good ever happens. And all this happens and everything's in this formula to keep you kind of bogged down in that mindset of just like when's the safe gonna drop on me or when's the safe gonna drop on other people around me and it just gives you this pending doom feeling. Because of that reason, I would say my t-shirt would say, if anybody out there could hate for any reason, and spew vomit in any of these online platforms or poison to anybody else; I would say 'Love for no Reason.' If you can hate for no reason, I say you could love for no reason. And that would be my t-shirt."

STACY JOHNSTON: "Would your t-shirt just say, 'Love for no reason,' or 'If you can hate for no reason you can love for no reason?'"

MIKE D'EGIDIO: "I mean I don't know. You could fit that on a t-shirt, I guess. In the short end, if you just wanted it simple you will put it on the front, put it on the back. I don't know the design. I'm not a not a marketeer, that's your department, but I would do, 'Love for no reason.' Wherever it came from, it doesn't matter. Love for no reason."

STACY JOHNSTON: "You know, one of the things that I have been the most honored in, in being able to do this podcast, and talk to the people that we have talked to, not only is it great to get your bits of gold and add to my candy dish and learn about your hero, and hope that people know what he means to you, see, because that means that's beautiful in itself. But it's the stories that you share with us on why that would be your statement, and then the statements themselves. It's my favorite part of this whole thing. I love the candy bowl additions and everything that comes along with it, but I really love the stories behind the t-shirts and behind the quotes, because they seem to be so genuine and so heartfelt and there's a lesson in every one of them. I could do half a day on love for no reason."

MIKE D'EGIDIO: "Yeah, no, absolutely."

BOYD HAMLIN: "I've got to jump in here real quick too and just add a couple of things because I want to marry two thoughts together, because I think it's just very, very good what we've been talking about Mike. This is what I've got written down. Serving is everything for others first. But your cup is never empty when you help others, and love for no reason. That is just a big challenge, you know, Stacy was talking earlier about her mind candy. This is like a feast for this coming year."

MIKE D'EGIDIO: "Yeah, it'll be, it will be, it's a continuum, you know. Even pre COVID it was important and now that COVID has kind of, you know, filtered through it. But I think it's only magnified that much more. I don't think I've forgotten that point and forgotten that essence, if not it's stronger now than it was pre COVID, honestly."

BOYD HAMLIN: "Oh absolutely. Very much, yes and we really appreciate you being on here today with us, Mike, and if somebody wanted to get in touch with you, and wanted to work with you in the area of real estate, things of that nature, how would they get in touch with you?"

MIKE D'EGIDIO: "I'm with the largest real estate company in the state of New Mexico, we've been number one for 40 years running, they can get me at coldwellbankerlegacy.com/mikedegidio, and they can also get to me on my website at abqhousebuying.com. They can reach out directly to me by phone. I'm also on Instagram at @ABQ House Buying. If you do any of the social media, the Instagram world seems to be very moot and very curt when it comes to the posting on there you don't find a whole lot of philosophical Mumbo stuff you kind of get to your point, tell your story, leave your prints, you know in your sentiment and kind of get out of there. So you guys can find me on there on Instagram anytime you reach out anytime to me."

BOYD HAMLIN: "Okay, thank you for sharing that because there's gonna be a lot of folks that are gonna want to reach out and work with somebody like you. That is very eager to work with them, and to help serve them in all ways that you possibly can. And as we just close out for our listeners today, one of the things that we want to reiterate is the time that we spent with Mike today. We want to help you understand that service is, in fact, everything. And to keep your cup full. Never, ever walk away from an opportunity to fill somebody else's cup and keep them thankful too. So with that in mind, we want to leave you with a challenge today, and it's going to be a challenge not just a week. I think it's going to be a challenge for your entire year to come. And here's the challenge- love for no reason at all. Thank you for joining us for the Hero Builder podcast. We look forward to our next episode, and our time together with you as our listeners. Thank you very much and we'll talk to you soon."

If a T-Shirt Could Talk...

Dear Reader:

To my un-caped heroes and readers:

In a modern, technology driven world it can be very hard for us to slow down individually as people. We have handfuls of devices keeping us linked in to communication streams constantly and our calendars are filled with events and activities sometimes for years in advance. These demands on our lives have changed the way we interact with the world around us and also how we as people collectively exchange ideas, principles, methods or any other types of information or data. The Un-Caped Heroes podcast has been an honor, privilege and blessing to be a part of as a direct source in exchanging with everyday people who do incredible things. Every day people seek to be the change they wish to see in the world and also encourage others on their journeys to do the very same.

For the readers of my small story, it was probably several months after I recorded the podcast that I saw my tee shirt slogan already used in the form of a book called "Love for no Reason" I was so very surprised (as many of us can be) when we see and are inundated with so much information it's very hard to tell where the original idea or slogan came from, but I welcomed the sentiment entirely as it is still the guiding principle of my life. I have to admit and be honest I really felt fraudulent and disingenuine that I had somehow stolen someone else's "phrase" or "slogan" that in a way I was cheapening their efforts of reaching and capitalizing on that sentiment while I was just merely feeling things from my heart. I think as everyday heroes and average people this could tend to hang us up for long periods of time and might take awhile to sift through those feelings, but I really had to sit with it hard upfront and be open to analyze my intentions around that phrase and maybe pressure myself to come up with something else. But honestly, after just reflecting on the existence of humanity and the short period of documented time that we've been on this earth, I feel like there are certain guiding truths and principles to everyone's life that they identify with and hold on to as part of the cores of our being and our own value system. These principles are ancient and they were meant to be shared. This struck a chord with me as I digested the very simplicity of the statement but also its complexity. As the universe and people collectively live within different vibration levels, I was finally able to reconcile the thought as merely complimentary being on the same vibration as the author. How truly special it was to have those words specifically in that order on my conscious and on the tip of my tongue when asked what my life's motto was.

    I believe we can get so caught up with originating and creating something ourselves that we forget that we co-exist with so many wonderful people around us and that humanity's greatest strength and asset lies within collaboration with each other. I hope those reading these stories are forever enriched, emboldened and encouraged to be open with yourself and to see the truth laid before you that as uncaped heroes we believe in you, we believe in your gifts and talents and we can't wait to read your story in how it all came together. I wish you nothing but love and light to your path and whether we connect in this world or the next I boldly encourage you always to love for no reason.

`MD

If a T-Shirt Could Talk...

CHRIS LUEHR

"Be the hero. Live your best story."

If a T-Shirt Could Talk...

About Me

Chris Luehr is a storyteller, attorney, professional speaker, coach, dinner-table comedian, and Minneapolis resident. His mission is to create joyful community through creating & laughing together. Whether speaking on a stage, arguing in a courtroom, or coaching in a boardroom, Chris enjoys connecting with people and helping them write their next chapter.

ChrisLuehr@gmail.con

Wisdom of Heroes

From Chris Luehr's Interview
(Episode #102)

STACY JOHNSTON: "So let's pretend this is your moment and the world is your audience. What's your statement, Chris, to the world? What does your t-shirt say?"

CHRIS LUEHR: "It's hard to put everything down into one line, but I think it's one of the beauties of a story. Kind of catch something in a story and people carry away with them their one line. And I've been thinking on it. My wife would tell me that I have plenty of words, more than plenty of words most of the time, and to try and to get that down to one phrase is a Herculean task, to say the least. But I think it would come down to something that I've already alluded to, and something that you talk about here. It's that often when people are talking about how to act they say, 'Don't be a hero.' They say, just play your role, don't be a hero. And I think again that gets to what you're talking about Stacy and Boyd, is that we have a misconception of what a hero really is. Someone who's trying to do it all by themselves. Someone who is trying to do it for the glory. And again, if you look at what a hero has been through the ages, a hero is someone who's dedicated to a higher purpose, and someone who is willing to work with allies, work with mentors, work with other people, that sort of real heroes. So I tell people, 'Be the hero. Live your best story.' That would be my line. Be the hero and live your best story. If you're really being a hero, what you're doing is you're answering that call inside of you, you're facing down your fears, going through a transformation and facing whatever that ugly thing is, and then bringing those lessons back. And we do this over and over again, if we have the courage to do it. Then, living your best story is the result of that work. So what I tell people is to go ahead, take the plunge. Be the hero, live your best story."

STACY JOHNSTON: "I think that is a perfect t-shirt. I have had so much fun with this question. It just sort of came to my mind one day and we decided to start using it. And we have so much fun with it. We get the most beautiful statements. We get the most powerful quotes that these people put on these t-shirts, but the stories behind them are powerful.

If a T-Shirt Could Talk...

So thank you for sharing them with us. One day I am going to have the coolest t-shirt wardrobe of anybody. I'm gonna have something to say everyday, right? I'm so excited about it. So thank you again for sharing it with us. I can't think of a better way to close out this day, to close out this conversation than to let you take the stage. How would you like to end and what would you say to our audience in your final words?"

CHRIS LUEHR: "First of all, I just want to say thanks again for this opportunity. It is connecting with other people that really makes whatever your journey is worthwhile. We have so much opportunity, so much ability to connect with other folks in the palm of our hand; but too often we use it to isolate and be individuals, so thanks for the chance to connect. And what I would encourage folks to do is to listen to whatever that call is. At first, it takes some time to get quiet. I was a very busy, very outgoing, very busy mind for many, many years and it wasn't until I got quiet, able to hear that voice inside and follow that voice. So I would say, answer that call, of whatever is calling you. Face those fears and continue your quest, because the everyday heroes are the people who get up and do it every single day. You'll have your moment of glory, you have your moment of transformation to have your moment, but the journey is about doing it every single day. So, continue your quest, and you will get to where you want to go and places that you've never even imagined."

Wisdom of Heroes

Dear Reader:

A hero doesn't seek out ticker tape parades. A hero sweeps up the street after the fanfar, silent & content in the work at hand. A hero doesn't hear the trumpets of victory or the shouts of adulation. A hero listens to the quiet cry for help. A hero does not boast or scribble the 10 Simple Steps of their success. A hero celebrates in silence, and then only for a moment, before focusing on the next single step in the journey. A hero does spoil for a fight. A hero seeks peace at all times, in all places. A hero does not seek the spotlight. A hero plays whatever role given, and plays it as best as they can. A hero is not born. A hero is created, through discipline, through humility, through experience. A hero should not be celebrated. A hero should be emulated. A hero is not someone, somewhere, out there. The hero lies within. The hero is you. The hero is always you. Live your best story. Be the hero.

If a T-Shirt Could Talk...

DR. GLORIA BURGESS

"Dream outside of the bulding!"

If a T-Shirt Could Talk...

About Me

Dr. Gloria J. Burgess is founding CEO of Jazz, Inc. and The Lift Every Voice Foundation, organizations that equip and inspire leaders throughout the world. A former executive in information technology, philanthropy, education, and human services, Gloria is a sought-after speaker, thought partner, and executive coach. She is a founding partner and serves as faculty with Maxwell Leadership, a global organization with members from over 140 countries. She also serves as executive leadership faculty at University of Washington, University of Southern California, Northwest University, Ghana's Sankofa Institute, and Slovenia's IEDC Bled School of Management.

Her recent books include Pass It On!, featuring her father's divinely-appointed relationship with Nobel Laureate William Faulkner, and Flawless Leadership: Connecting Who You Are with What You Know and Do. Gloria hosts a weekly podcast called "Legacy Living." Her popular leadership and personal growth programs include "A Seat at the Table," "Legacy Living," "Leading with Purpose and Passion," and "Flawless Leadership."

You can connect with Gloria at gloriaburgess.com

From Dr. Gloria Burgess' Interview
(Episode #106)

STACY JOHNSTON: "Gloria, with all that you've shared and all that you know and all of your life experience. If this was your moment, and the world was watching, and this was your platform; what would your t-shirt say when you walked out on stage?"

DR. GLORIA BURGESS: "You know what my t-shirt would say is, 'Dream outside of the building' Not outside of the box, but dream outside of the building. In other words, dream big. That will be on the front, Stacy, and on the back is, 'Ask somebody to help you.' Because a dream that big can't be done just by you, it can't be achieved alone. So bring somebody with you. Bring many somebodies with you. We need to collaborate with other people, and know that we are not alone. We don't have to do this dreaming alone, and certainly not achieving that size dream alone."

STACY JOHNSTON: "That's beautiful. I think that's beautiful. Dream outside the building. You know we always hear outside the box and I myself am not a box girl. I don't like the box, I don't live in the box. I stay outside the box, so to get permission to dream outside the building, not just the box is super freeing for me. I love that idea. Boyd and I have talked again many times during recording this podcast that when you look at children, and you look at how they come somewhere along the way, they've shut the wonder down. When I watch my grandchildren I see that fascination and the wonder that they have about the world around us. And at some point we tell them, don't ask so many questions, so we shut that wonder down. Then we find ourselves later in their life trying to teach them how to dream again. So if there was a place in the middle where we didn't stop the wonder. I think that one of the joys of being a grandparent is that we get to absorb the wonder. Because it's not our job to make the dentist appointments, or make sure the science project is on time, we get the wonder, and it's totally a gift for me."

If a T-Shirt Could Talk...

Dear Reader:

I know we talked a little bit before the show began and we talked about that ordinary person doing the extraordinary. And all of us are ordinary people. We have pedestals that we put people on; but we're all ordinary people. And just know, know that you can do whatever you set out to do, and know that it's not about you. It's about helping to make the world a better place. So again I'm going to say link elbows with somebody and bring somebody with you, do not go it alone. So know that you can do it. Know that you need somebody else to help you to walk with you along the way, we are building a relationship.

WILLIAM BROWN

"So go be you."

About Me

William Brown
The "Real You" Finder
Coach, Speaker, Retreat Facilitator and Author
Founder of Living Beyond
Email- livingbeyondgroup@gmail.com

Mailing Address
9900 Poplar Tent Rd Ste. 115 PMB 210
Concord, NC 28027

Social Media
Facebook Page- @livingbeyondgroup
Facebook Group -@thegroundedmonk
LinkedIn-iamwilliam
Instagram- @livingbeyondgroups

Children's Books
Beyond the Shell- Finding You Beyond what Protects You
Beyond the Shell- The Journey to Stay You
Both available on Amazon
For Coaching schedule your Label Finder Exploratory Call - https://calendly.com/livingbeyond/exploratory

From William Brown's Interview
(Episode #108)

STACY JOHNSTON: Let's pretend this is your moment. You're on the stage, you walk out and take the platform. The world is your stage. What does your t-shirt say?

WILLIAM BROWN: "'So go be you.' I think the more that we really embrace that being myself and being yourself is the only way to really show up in the world. That's all that you can do. Nothing else is necessary. So on my shirt, it would just say; so, with everything else that's going on in your life. Be you. Just go and be you. That's what I want people to embrace and kind of be afraid of and be excited about, and just live that the rest of their life."

STACY JOHNSTON: "I think that's beautiful."

If a T-Shirt Could Talk...

Dear Reader:

There have been a number of gifts in 2020, and sometimes with the gifts that we get, we don't understand why we're getting the gift, or if we should be getting the gifts. And so, the gift of the pandemic and a lot of things that have caused us to stop in our tracks to see what's important is an opportunity to see who we are and how we're going to show up for each other. And it is my prayer that 2021 is not reinforcing who you are, But having the doing and who you are. And so, you can do all the things that you believe that this time is calling you to do, because now you know who you are and what's important to you.

DREW GERALD

"Make truth the most important thing."

If a T-Shirt Could Talk...

About Me

Drew Gerald is an American author, entrepreneur, and director at the Center for Cinesomatic Development. He founded Cinesomatics, a healing technology leading the world in cinematic movement diagnostics and graduate-level consciousness studies. Drew holds workshops internationally from New York to London, Tuscany to Switzerland, as well as virtually; integrating embodiment, spirituality, video, shadow work, trauma therapy, and feeling-based awareness.

His first teaching, Holistic Sex, introduced a new paradigm that bridged the divide sexuality, spirituality, and the sexes. Earlier in his career, Drew coded a particle and physics engine by age 18, used by top fortune 100 companies over the 7 years of his software business.

A spiritual advisor and healer to some of the world's most successful, Andrew works with clients one-on-one and in intimate groups. His graduate-level programs of consciousness studies offer memberships to deep transformational classes that bridge the teachings of the ancient mysteries with modern psychology and technology.

Andrew is also an active advisor to the official Alan Watts Organization.

Visit and learn more about Drew @ drewgerald.com

Wisdom of Heroes

From Drew Gerald's Interview
(Episode #112)

STACY JOHNSTON: "Okay, Drew…So with all this gold was laid before us. If this was your moment and the world was your stage, and you have a chance to make a statement to the world. What is your one liner or what would your T-shirt say?"

DREW GERALD: "Make truth the most important thing."

STACY JOHNSTON: "That's beautiful. You want to expand on that for us?"

DREW GERALD: "So this ties in with the heroic life and with the avoidant life because we all make our life stand for something. And so many of us don't even know what that is. What our life stands for is not something that we have in our head. It's the universe around us. I can tell you what you stand for based on the choices you make and how you show up in the world. So we can have an internal idea of what we think we stand for , but that really doesn't matter compared to the reality and the results of how we've shown up in the world. And so making the truth the most important thing, you can't go wrong with it. If you make happiness the most important thing, you're going to suffer a lot because life is not about being happy 100% of the time. Not only is it not what it's about, you wouldn't want that. It's like listening to the C major chord being played for 20 minutes straight, you'd go crazy. So, if you make your life about anything that's not true, or real, such as avoidance or suffering, or victim mentality, or disease or laziness or whatever it is, you're going to come up against some trouble. And so I found that if you make truth, even beyond being nice, even beyond being a good person, because sometimes the truth isn't a nice thing to tell somebody, but the truth is always loving. Now, if it's not loving, it's not the truth. So if we can orient ourselves towards the truth, then it's really hard to go astray. Now you may come up against some friction, right? You may bump up against other people that don't put the truth as the most important thing and so you've got to deal with some stuff. But I've found nothing beyond the truth to make the important thing because to me, the truth is love. Love is the truth. Telling the truth is loving to self and others and love is true. So, along those lines, you have things like beauty, enjoyment and playfulness, compassion, gratitude. Those are all very important things. Those are great things to stand for. But to me above all else, when we can orient ourselves to the truth you know, our true north star so to speak. It's really almost impossible to go astray."

STACY JOHNSTON: "What a beautiful statement, and what a beautiful goal to actually make truth the most important thing because it's pretty easy in the world right now to look around and make lots of other things important. And we hide the truth so many times."

Dear Reader:

Andrew Daniel is an award-winning author, spiritual teacher, and director at the Center for Cinesomatic Development. He is the founder of Cinesomatics®—a feeling-based therapy utilizing video feedback and movement to assess and resolve stuck somatic, psychological, and emotional patterns. This work is held online and in-person internationally, from NY to London, Tuscany to Switzerland.

His latest book, Awaken to Your True Self (MetaHeal), is a recipient of the 2022 gold Nautilus Book Awards. This definitive guide helps self-aware entrepreneurs, artists, professionals, and leaders break through stuck cycles and genuinely wake up.

A spiritual advisor and healer to some of the world's most successful, Andrew works with clients one-on-one and in intimate groups. His graduate-level programs of consciousness studies offer memberships to deep transformational classes that bridge the teachings of the ancient mysteries with modern psychology and technology.

Andrew is also an active advisor to the official Alan Watts Organization.

If a T-Shirt Could Talk...

CHRIS GORDON

"Pass on perfection— go for greatness!"

If a T-Shirt Could Talk...

About Me

Chris DT Gordon is a faithful husband, father of three, online middle school special education teacher, professional speaker, podcast host, co-author, runner, 1st Degree Black Belt in Tae Kwon Do, and pop culture geek. He is also a survivor of necrotizing fasciitis (flesh-eating bacteria) who uses his story and message to inspire high school students and other young adults to adopt The Attitude of Gratitude (TAG), overcome their "personal bacteria", increase their positivity and gratitude, and make the world around them a better place!

Email: chris@chrisdtgordon.com
Website: chrisdtgordon.com

Check out what Chris has to offer as a speaker, download a free TAG one sheet, watch and/or listen to the Scar Bearers podcast, read some of his articles, visit his merch store to snag some fun and inspiring wearables, and more!

Instagram: @chrisdtgordon

From Chris Gordon's Interview
(Episode #115)

STACY JOHNSTON: "Chris, when you look at all the conversation that we've had and where you've been. If this is your moment, and you have an opportunity, and the world is your stage. When you take that stage, Chris, what's your one liner to the world? What does your t-shirt say?"

CHRIS GORDON: "My t-shirt says, 'Pass on perfection, and go for greatness.' Because I look at myself in the mirror, and I'll tell you guys, like I said, I'm a mess. I have scars all over the right side of my body, I'm missing a nipple. I didn't say that before, but when I go to the beach I look like I'm winking at everyone. I have a huge scar going down my left thigh. It's just not pretty. It's not perfect, but it's great. I work out every day. I push myself to the limit. I set high goals for myself to see what I can accomplish, and know that I will never look perfect. I will never be perfect. But if I stay committed and consistent and do the best that I can, I will always be great."

BOYD HAMLIN: "That is really good. Stacy, is that kind of what you were thinking that you were going to get? Or does that just blow you out of the water?"

STACY JOHNSTON: "That just blew me away. That just kind of blew me away a little bit. Pass on perfection and go for greatness. We're so conditioned in the society that we live in that perfection is what we have to strive for. And we leave greatness behind so many times in that way. So Chris, I've had a beautiful time today with this conversation and I'm so appreciative of your perspective and your attitude. I'm all over the superhero costume. I think that is the coolest thing I've heard all day. You dress in costumes and go to town, I love it! So, I cannot think of a better way Chris to close out this show, then to give you the stage for 60 seconds. What is the last thing, what would you like to leave our audience with today, to drive home your points?"

CHRIS GORDON: "Well, besides passing on perfection going for greatness, I would like them to look around their house. I want them to notice seemingly insignificant items that may be around their person. Be it a pen or a post it note or a chair. Think about how those items have served them, especially when they needed them most. We all know the feeling of needing a pen and miraculously or out of some divine intervention, one's not there. You are desperately searching for one, then all of a sudden you find it, and you are filled with joy at this little device that can now help you accomplish your goal. Instead of feeling gratitude for that at that moment feel gratitude for it now, when you have it. And do that for as many things in your house and you will find yourself to be as rich as someone who has a full bank account. And if you live your life like that, you will find more happiness, more joy, more appreciation for everything and everyone around you."

Dear Reader:

First of all, thank you so much for reading this! I may never meet you, virtually or in-person, so please know that my connection with you is one filled with gratitude.

Whenever I share my message, whether it's in a podcast interview (like the one I experienced with Stacy and Boyd), or I'm speaking to an audience, I strive to increase others' gratitude, positivity, and resilience. We all face struggles that test our physical, spiritual, emotional, and/or mental mettle. Those struggles could be daily, periodic, or once-in-a-lifetime. No matter their occurrence rate, they have the capability to change our lives.

The only thing you need to remember when you're facing those situations is this: "Where your thoughts go, your mind and body will follow." If you develop or accept positive thoughts, you create a positive mindset and take positive actions. The same is true for negative thoughts. By starting with a place of authentic gratitude, you will more likely handle and overcome the obstacle with greater positivity and resilience, making you stronger on the other side. Whatever you face, please know that you are not alone, even if you are by yourself. Please reach out to me if you wish to connect, either to establish a connection or increase your gratitude. Thanks again for being here. Now, pass on perfection, and go for greatness!

Chris DT Gordon

If a T-Shirt Could Talk...

STAR HANSEN

"Love your chaos."

About Me

Star Hansen brings peace to the world one color-coded label at a time. Known as the "Clutter Whisperer," Star's multi-layered approach is that of mind, body, spirit, & space. Star has a knack for seeing through the chaos and into the lives & hearts of those she works with. Through her unique approach, she diagnoses people's emotional and lifestyle blocks, guiding them to a state of organization and joy. She has been featured on OWN, TLC, HGTV, Style, and A&E. Star's thought-provoking TEDx talk explores what the monsters in your closet are trying to tell you. Star lives in Tucson, AZ and can be found helping people across the world shift their relationship to clutter through her Chaos to Calm Organizing Community.

Website: www.starhansen.com
Email: star@starhansen.com

Wisdom of Heroes

From Star Hansen's Interview
(Episode #117)

STAR HANSEN: "So one of the questions y'all asked is if I had something written on a t-shirt what would it be? And I would say, 'Love your chaos.' Chaos is not something that should be shunned, ashamed of, we have those feelings about it. But the truth is chaos is created, chaos is creation energy. And so when you look at the chaos and wildness around you, like yes it can suck the oxygen out of the room, but it can also contain in it the pieces that build your life. The building blocks that are building your tomorrow, and who you will be, and who you are. It brings all of that together and the desire to love it, so you can masterfully see what's in there and pull what you want. Shop from your chaos so that you can build the life that is meant for you to have the greatest joy and happiness and expression of the being that you came to be."

Closing Statement: "I mean, I think that for sure fear, shame, guilt, whatever we were handed in this life, whatever our emotional dance partner is that we've come to kind of tango with in this lifetime, that is what is buried in your clutter. That for sure stops us. The way that I suggest for people to start to come in harmony with your home is like to create. Think of it not of a purging, a removal, but a creation. If you were creating your home, I want you to walk into your home and to know instantaneously that you, and only you, could live there. Have it be so personal, and so you, because when we have that space set up in that way, we are at home. We are safe. We are open. The rest of the world could be falling down, but in your home you have safety. For us to get there, we have to dance with those big feelings. We have to meet our fear face to face, and not say get out of here; or I'm going to hide you with alcohol or I'm going to run the other way. But to learn to accept that these feelings are a part of the journey. That it is not a matter of "oh when I get better this fear will never come up again." You want fear. You want to walk down a dark valley, and know if you should be paying better attention in the valley, right? You want to be able to feel elation when you're dancing with someone you love and playing, right? You want all the feelings, you just want to pick. You want to be the captain of that ship. What we want to do is instead of choosing to 'oh these don't belong here, I shouldn't be feeling this' and hiding, to embrace because that fear you feel around the clutter is the thing we're healing. We're healing the clutter, but really we're (healing) the fear that causes the clutter to competuate. Being present to yourself, a mindful practice as simple as breathing in "I'm aware that I feel fear" breathing out 'I care for that fear.' Then just repeating that until you get to a calmer state is kind of all you need. Just the small things to remove the bigger feelings that stop us from making progress. Simple is always better when it comes to solutions."

Dear Reader:

If you're struggling with the clutter and chaos in your life, please know you're not alone. There are countless people that feel the same way you do. The good news is that the chaos may not be what you think. Contrary to the negative voices in our heads, the chaos of your life isn't trying to tell you that there's something wrong with you. It's an invitation to expand into the next version of yourself. The "stuff" is here because you're ready for your next chapter. It's time. It's your time. And you don't have to do it alone. If you want to use your clutter as the catalyst for transformation into the next version of you, come to www.starhansen.com. Let me help you discover what your clutter is trying to tell you.

With Love and Gratitude,
Star Hansen
Clutter Whisperer
www.starhansen.com

If a T-Shirt Could Talk...

CELIA KIBLER

"Laughter. It really is the best medicine."

If a T-Shirt Could Talk...

About Me

Celia Kibler is a best-selling author, a Family Empowerment Coach and the Founder of Pumped Up Parenting, Funfit® Family Fitness, and International Day of Calm. She is the Mom of 5 kids; 2 she gave birth to & 3 she gained from marriage; as well as a Grandma of 9. She has successfully parented a blended family for over 24 years. Celia is on a Mission to stop 1,000,000 Parents from Yelling at Their Kids. Her book, RAISING HAPPY TODDLERS: How to Build Great Parenting Skills and Stop Yelling at Your Kids is available for purchase from Amazon in Kindle and paperback. She has written 3 children's books to enhance the development of kids... BEING DIFFERENT IS FUN, I AM GRATEFUL & ALL ABOUT ME. Celia believes that the more parents understand their children and themselves, the better they can communicate and relate while building trust and respect within a nurturing, fun environment. Her reason is simple... because we are raisingadults, not children.

With over 40 years of coaching, teaching, and counseling kids and their parents, including Special Needs populations, Celia has found successful solutions for real-life parenting situations with advice that is easy to follow, doable, and result-driven. She brings that wisdom to you in her book, as well as in Private and Group Coaching programs.
Phone: +1-301-922-2164 | Email: celia@pumpedupparenting.com
facebook.com/celia.kibler @parenting_expert_toddlers
Websites: pumpedupparenting.com | TalkWithCelia.com

Wisdom of Heroes

From Celia Kibler's Interview
(Episode #120)

STACY JOHNSTON: "Okay Celia. Let's take this chance. Let's pretend like this is your moment, and the world is your stage. When you walk out, what's your one liner to the world, Celia? What's your t-shirt say?"

CELIA KIBLER: "'Laughter. It really is the best medicine.' I say it every time I do anything, I end everything with it. You gotta laugh! Stuff is funny! Laugh at yourself, laugh at other people, laugh at situations, make jokes. Have fun. Laugh. Laughter is great exercise number one, and a great stress reducer, and a great way to connect with other people. You've got to laugh. Stuff is funny. Stuff is really funny and people are really funny. So laugh. A lot."

STACY JOHNSTON: "I think you're so right. I think that there's healing in laughter, meaning when you go through a process and you get to a place in your life that you can actually come back and have some humor in it, then you know the healing is real. If we could just learn to laugh along the way, it wouldn't take so long to get better from it. If you look at your situation and just kind of laugh and go, 'Well, I guess this is what we'll do today instead.' Right? Because you're in it anyway. Your attitude and your level of love while you are in it has such an effect on the outcome of the situation."

CELIA KIBLER: "Absolutely. You know Alan Alda said a funny quote that I read somewhere. He said, 'When people are laughing, they don't want to kill each other.' And that's the truth! When you're laughing, you're feeling good. Those chemicals in your brain are churning and making you happy. So that's my quote."

STACY JOHNSTON: "What a great Facebook quote. What a great Monday morning quote for Facebook!"

CELIA KIBLER: "I was going to put it in my book, but then people were like 'don't put that in your book.' Well, you know?"

If a T-Shirt Could Talk...

STACY JOHNSTON: "Oh that would totally go in mine. I think that's a great quote. I was an Alda fan when I was a kid. My parents would make us go in the other room so they could watch M*A*S*H*. We were cracking the door, right?"

CELIA KIBLER: "We still, actually I think my husband and I watched M*A*S*H* just the other day."

STACY JOHNSTON: "We watch it every once in a while on the old TV show channel. Same channel Andy Griffith comes on. Celia, I can't think of a better way to close out this podcast than to tell you thank you so much for your time, for your information, for your knowledge, for the books that you brought , for the information you share for the people that you touch. If you have any questions about how to reach her, please reach out to us at herobuilder2020@gmail.com And if you don't mind I would love to close with your quote, laughter really is the best medicine."

Wisdom of Heroes

Dear Reader:

Thank you for reading the messages in this book. I hope you are taking a lot of this advice with you throughout your day. I wanted to spend a little more time talking about my message and my mission in this world.

You see, my entire life has been dedicated to the health and wellness of children. In 1987, I started Funfit® Family Fitness to give kids the joy of physical fitness, without the stress and often insecurities that are found in competitive sports. In 2016, I decided to continue empowering kids, by empowering their parents to create peaceful, cooperative, respectful, and fun households, and started Pumped Up Parenting. Then I decided to get on a mission to stop 1,000,000 parents from yelling at their kids… why, because we're raising adults, not children. When we yell consistently to a child, we create a child that becomes afraid of us, not one that respects us as so many parents believe. Just ask yourself if you respect a person that consistently yells at you.

Yelling and aggression creates many changes in a child, and I will be willing to bet that if you were yelled at as a child, you will relate to some, if not all, of these outcomes. A child that lives with yelling and aggression, becomes fearful, believes that nothing they do is good enough, believes that they can't do anything right, believes that they are not worthy, they lack confidence and self-esteem, and the very sad reality is that they don't grow to hate their parents, they grow to hate themselves. These affects don't just go away, they stay with us forever unless we work to reverse them. Wouldn't it be phenomenal to create the next generation of adults who don't have to recover from their childhoods?

Can you imagine the difference in this world? Well, I thought a lot about that too and made it my mission to help as many parents as I can to make a difference in their child's life. I wrote a manual for parents (since most believe one doesn't come with their child), Raising Happy Toddlers: How to Build Great Parenting Skills and Stop Yelling at Your Kids, so they can find positive, successful, loving solutions to their everyday challenges. I've written 3 children's books (with more to come) and I am determined to do what I need to do, to reach as many parents as possible. Then I thought, "Why stop with parents?" Why not work to get all humans to become more intentional with their behavior, their reactions, their personal development, and emotional regulation. Why not have a day where everyone can feel like their own hero and a hero to someone else?

A hero is any person that is kind, compassionate, thoughtful, respectful, and encouraging to others, but it starts with that person having all those qualities for themselves so that they can give to others. An angry, stressed-out person cannot possibly offer anything up to another, except more anger and more stress. So where do we start, how do we de-stress and find our calm? I knew people needed answers and much sooner than later. So again, I decided, to expand my reach and help even more people.

I created the International Day of Calm (DayofCalm.org), an annual day on April 5th, when everyone can choose to stay calm for just 24 hours. My hope is that one day of calm will make people feel so good, that they will continue to stay calm for days to come. A day full of free classes that focus on different areas of life that may be causing undue stress and that will help someone learn to feel calmer. A day when you can intentionally choose how you react to situations and other people, choosing not to yell but talk calmly, choosing not to judge or criticize but understand and listen, choosing to stop hating and instead start loving and learning about someone who does not think or live the same way you do. To start making a choice about how you live your life in a world full of people that also need to live their lives; all different but so much the same. Similar dreams, similar hopes, so many more similarities than differences. Giving everyone the right to live happily ever after, not just in a fairy tale but in their own real world.

So where can you start, what can you do to start living a happier, more positive, calmer, less stressful life? Here are some action steps you can do today.

1. Review your life, that's right, take a long look. Write down what is

stressing you out and usually the first thing that comes to mind, is where you need to start. Is it your job, your family, your partner, your home, your beliefs, the News, the world, your fears…what is it?
2. Once you have pin-pointed where you need to start, try to figure out what about it is stressing you out.
3. Think about what it will mean to you to resolve this daily tension and frustration.
4. Now ask yourself, "Do I need help?" If the answer is "yes," start reaching out. Who can help you with changing what's going on? If you don't need help to resolve it, then start with baby steps. 10 minutes a day, every day, may be all you need to work on resolving the issue.
5. Be intentional, be consistent and be persistent… calming your life may save your life.

I said as my quote on the Everyday Heroes Podcast, that "Laughter is the best medicine." It really is. Laughter relieves stress, it breathes new life into your lungs, it stimulates your heart, it exercises your body, it increases the endorphins in your brain, it increases your immunity and makes you healthier.

What if you could laugh more? What if you were able to find a mistake humorous, instead of beating yourself or someone else up, over it? What if you were able to walk away from a conflict and think about how you are going to react to it, instead of just exploding without thinking? What if you found things funny, instead of taking life so seriously? What if you found your fun?

What if? I challenge you to join my mission to stop yelling at your kids, to stop over-reacting, to stop creating more chaos, to start thinking before you react, so that you are the calming element in the situation. How would that make you feel? No one that I've met feels good when they yell and in fact, they all tell me they feel like a bad parent, a bad friend, a bad person. This is our one life. It is not a dress rehearsal, and no one is getting out of here alive. What if you could make it a life that makes you feel proud of yourself every day?

If a T-Shirt Could Talk...

Ask yourself, if you were to die tomorrow, what would your child say about how you parented them. Would others feel a void in their lives because you're no longer around? How would you want to be remembered? I beg of you not to wait. Decide to change. Decide to be the best version of you, you can be. Decide to become your own hero. You're the deciding vote in your life. You're the one that can change your world. Can you imagine, if each person makes the same decision to live their best life, to stop all the hatred, criticism and judgement and just start to believe more in themselves and others? I believe we really can change this world right now and for generations to come. Why, because it's contagious.

Let's replace this pandemic, with the pandemic of becoming intentionally calmer and happier. It all starts with just one person…YOU! Think more, dream more, smile more, laugh more…it really is the best medicine.

Sending you peace and love!

Celia

JAKE DOHERTY

"Keep your options open."

If a T-Shirt Could Talk...

About Me

I was looking for the perfect birthday gift for my mom. She had spent a great deal of time in her life as a talented cook, entertaining and gifting people with her skill. It brought her such joy. Then, in 2018, she suffered a stroke that took her left hand mobility and her ability to cook. This was life changing for her.

Boyd and I were gifted with the opportunity to interview Jake for the Everyday Heroes section of our show just about this time. He gave a delightful interview filled with emotion and a tangible passion for his work and service. Living in Germany, Jake has served our Troops and families abroad in multiple ways. And now he serves in a new way.

During the course of the pandemic, Jake found himself in a position to create a new company called "Dari Deri." This fabulous business is comprised of multiple talented chef's from all over that create virtual cooking experiences. I was intrigued in a special way. This was the perfect gift for my mom.

For years, she and her husband had participated in a thing called 'A Date For 8.' This was four couples that got together once a month for a dinner party, taking turns hosting and cooking for each other. Through Jake, DeriDari, our delightful chef, and this fabulous program, we were able to create a virtual cooking experience for my mom with the ladies from her Date for 8 group. The chef walked us all through the experience from " Good afternoon ladies and welcome to your kitchen" to plating her birthday dinner. It was such an amazing experience for us all. You can find out more about the amazing experience options available by visiting: Deridari.com

Thank you, Jake
Stacy Johnston

From Jake Doherty's Interview
(Episode #127)

STACY JOHNSTON: "If this was your opportunity and you have a moment to make a statement to the world. What's your one line, Jake? What does your t-shirt say?"

JAKE DOHERTY: "Wow. Honestly, I have to go back to my mother. Since I was a young child she was such an inspiration, able to not only care for me, but also to live such an amazing life, to walk a path that she said she could. So I'm going to honor her, and I'm going to do so by saying my one line is, as I've already said, 'Keep your options open.'"

STACY JOHNSTON: "That's beautiful. And in keeping your options open, Jake, where has that taken you?"

JAKE DOHERTY: "For me, it's taken me all over the world. It has taken me into many different industries and many different paths. But in the end, it has brought me to where I need to be. Here in this little town of Garmisch-Partenkirchen, Germany, with my beautiful wife and my two gorgeous daughters. And I actually live in a little neighborhood where I haven't locked the back door since I moved in, and I get to walk out in my backyard and hike up a mountain anytime I want. I live in a culture that I just absolutely admire. I admire the Bavarians, they are just so unique. So if you keep your options open, spiritually, mentally, you never know what you're going to achieve."

STACY JOHNSTON: "I can't think of a better way to leave today than that thought. Right? How many times do we close off those doors because we think there's no room for my idea and nobody wants to hear what I have to say. So we close those doors for ourselves and we eliminate our very own options. What sound and wise advice."

If a T-Shirt Could Talk...

Dear Reader:

Well you just said closing doors because of fear. And I'm going to do something that's kind of odd. I'm going to quote a TV show. That TV show is Star Trek Discovery. I just watched the last episode of that TV show, and the Captain came on in this very serious moment and he grabbed his crew, and he wanted to impart strong words; a strong sentiment. And it was honestly very touching for me especially in my current struggles of having to close one business and open a new door. I was scared and filled with fear everyday that I was going to let these chefs down. That I am going to financially destroy my family, not be able to send my kids to college or put food on my table. But, I have to keep moving forward. The Captain of Star Trek Discovery came out and said something, and it brought me to tears. He said, "even in fear we can step forward." And that's become my current motto with the stresses and trials and tribulations of having a startup and trying to not only start a business, but one that a lot of people are relying on. These chefs, they're just simply trying to keep food on their tables. And so there's a lot of pressure ensuring that I can make that happen. So even in fear I can step forward.

SAPNA RADHAKRISHNAN

"Do the work."

If a T-Shirt Could Talk...

About Me/Contact Me

Website: sapnarad.com

Facebook and Instagram: @sapnaradcoaching

From Sapna Radhakrishnan's Interview
(Episode #130)

STACY JOHNSTON: "Sapna, let's take it to this place…let's say that the world is your stage, you have this one moment of golden opportunity to make a statement to the entire world. What's your one liner, Sapna? What does your T-shirt say?"

SAPNA RAD: "I would say, 'Do the Work.' It's not as scary as you think it is. Marriage is hard; so is divorce. Being single is hard, having four children to feed is hard. Being healthy is hard. You have to work out, you have to eat right. Being overweight and having difficulty walking is hard. Nobody has it easy, nobody has it easy. We all are in this together. We all are."

STACY JOHNSTON: "That's huge."

SAPNA RAD: "That's what I would like to say, we all are in this. Let's do the work."

STACY JOHNSTON: "'Do the work.' And you know, we talk about work ethic and we talk about getting up everyday to go to work. But this work is the work you don't talk about at parties, right? It's the work that we hide and the work that we pretend like is not ours to do. So, I love that. I think that this statement, 'Do the Work' has so much power behind it, and is a complete conversation starter. I love it! So, Sapna as we get ready to close out for the day I want to tell you thank you again. And can you tell me where are you from? Where do you provide these services from? Where are you home based?"

SAPNA RAD: "I live in Dallas, but my programs are all online, they are eight weeks, they're online, they can sign up and they can work at their own pace. And I'm there with them, guiding them for the whole eight weeks. It's all online. There's no pressure. They just need to have the will to have better connections. To heal. That's all it requires."

STACY JOHNSTON: "Perfect. Sapna as we get ready to close, I can't think

of a better way to close than to give you the stage for sixty seconds. Please, leave us with some final words of golden encouragement for our audience."
SAPNA RAD: "Going back to what I said before, it is about doing the work. We have to do this work now, or 10 years later. Let's do it now. We're all in this together. If we help each other, we're gonna get there sooner. And this story that the mind might say, "that you're alone in this", well don't believe that! It's not true. These are all lies that we have been told and we believe. Let's do the work. Let's heal. Let's heal ourselves, our family, and the planet."

Wisdom of Heroes

Dear Reader:

Going back to what I said before, it is about doing the work. We have to do this work now, or 10 years later. Let's do it now. We're all in this together. If we help each other, we're gonna get there sooner. And this story that the mind might say, "that you're alone in this", well don't believe that! It's not true. These are all lies that we have been told and we believe. Let's do the work. Let's heal. Let's heal ourselves, our family, and the planet.

If a T-Shirt Could Talk...

RAYNA NEISES

HERO

"It might be hard, but it will be worth it!"

About Me

Rayna Neises is the author of No Regrets: Hope for Your Caregiving Season, an International Coach Federation certified coach, Independent Certified Positive Approach to Care® Trainer, the host of "A Season of Caring Podcast, and speaker who is passionate about supporting daughters and sons in a season of caring with their aging parents. Rayna lost both of her parents to Alzheimer's disease twenty years apart. After her season of caring for her dad through his journey, she founded A Season of Caring Coaching where she offers regret-free resources, encouragement, and support aimed at preventing family caregivers from aimlessly wandering through this important season of life. Rayna lives on a farm in southeast Kansas with her husband, Ron, and a small pack of adorable dogs. She is the baby of her family, but most would never guess. She is a former teacher and small business owner. Rayna enjoys crafts of all kinds and spending time with her grandkids most of all.

Phone: 620-921-0082
Email: Rayna@ASeasonofCaring.com
Websites: www.ASeasonOfCaring.com | www.noregrets-book.com

Wisdom of Heroes

From Rayna Neises' Interview
(Episode #133)

STACY JOHNSTON: "Rayna, when we look at you, and this beautiful story that you have, and this legacy that you leave of love. If you had an opportunity, and if the world was your stage, you had their attention. What is your one line statement to the world, Rayna? What does your t-shirt say?"

RAYNA NEISES: "It might be hard, but it'll be worth it."

STACY JOHNSTON: That's beautiful. Can you expand on that for us?

RAYNA NEISES: "Sure. I think that every season of life has hard stuff. And that as a person whose had both of her parents forget who she is, have a change in personality, not be able to care for themselves for extended periods of time. You know, it was hard, but it was so worth it. And I just think that challenging people to really understand how valuable those relationships are, and how important our family is to us. We really, even in the middle of the hard, you just need to keep in mind, it really is worth it."

STACY JOHNSTON: "That's so beautiful. That is so gorgeous. Thank you. What a beautiful t-shirt. One of the things I have enjoyed the very most about this podcast is; we've done what Boyd, 125 interviews at this point? And not one statement has repeated itself. With that many of the most gorgeous heartfelt, here's my passion statement to the world. Coolest t-shirt ever Rayna. Thank you for sharing that with us. And what a beautiful thought that it might be hard, but it'll all be worth it. Rayna as we get ready to close I can't think of a better way than to give you the stage and let you share your last bit of gold with us. So, what would you like to leave our audience with today?"

RAYNA NEISES: "Really just embrace the moment which we've talked a lot about. Treasure what you have and embrace the moment. There is hope even in the middle of caregiving and all of the things that come along with it. Really being able to bury your parents with no regrets is a tall order, but

If a T-Shirt Could Talk...

I think it is one that is doable. Really being intentional with your time and your support event as they age, and just being able to step into it will be something you won't regret. So I just want to challenge and encourage the listeners to think about how they can do that with their parents, if their parents already passed, with their siblings and other family members, even those who are just neighbors, but special people that come into our lives for a reason. Just really treasure that time and focus in on what you can do, how you can give and support and be able to look back without regret."

Wisdom of Heroes

Dear Reader:

If you are like me and both of your parents have already passed from this life to the next, it might have been a while since you have thought of yourself as a daughter or son. Or, if you have not faced the season of walking your parent all the way home yet, I want to encourage you to spend time thinking about the many memories you have made with them throughout your life.

There is something special about being a daughter or a son. Even if your upbringing was difficult, your parents are unlike anyone else on earth. I have heard a parent's love described as the only people in this world who cannot see us unbiasedly. That was my experience as they always saw the best and wanted the best for me.

We all know that no one lives forever but if your parents are still living, have you thought about what you might wish you had or had not done once your parent is no longer here?

It is not something anyone likes to think about, but I want to challenge you to do just that. The only way to find yourself at the grave of your parent without regrets is to be determined to make the decisions you need to get there. You will not wander onto this path. Wanderings lead to resentment, guilt, and regret.

The end of life is much like the beginning because the need for care is extremely high as our independence diminishes with time. It is no doubt uncomfortable to see those who raised us and taught us so much in a place of needing support and care. Coming alongside your parent now, learning their likes and dislikes from an adult perspective, and having the difficult conversations now will mean so much to you later.

Whether you find yourself in a place where you do the hands-on caregiving, you are a long-distance caregiver, or you are supporting them in a nursing facility, you will become their caregiver, and this will be a hard season. It is important not to do this season alone. You are your parent's

If a T-Shirt Could Talk...

legacy. They do not want you to give up your life and health to care for them. They want you to live a life you love while supporting them while they age.

I found that building a team to support me and my family was one of the keys to having no regrets. Hiring help so that I could continue to care for my husband and son, work my business, and care for myself was important. Each person on our team brought a different skill set and personality when caring for my dad. I created a quiz to help you explore your caring personality. Learning your strengths and weaknesses can help you discover what you do well and who you might need to hire to complete your team. You can take it for free at www.caringquiz.com.

Another key to burying my dad with no regrets was the intentional act of finding the good. During my caring season, I was able to spend more time with my dad than I had since I was a child. Yes, there were caregiving tasks that needed to be done such as cooking, medication administration, and protecting him from all that he did not understand but there were also moments that became cherished memories. Moments of laughter, compassion, and joy from the time we spent playing Ping-Pong, going to the gym to work out, completing puzzles, cleaning up the yard, bowling, and singing our hearts out to Nate King Cole. This season can be harder than you can imagine. It will hurt more than you expect but it will also be filled with sweet moments if you look for them.

There are many hard things in life. The season of walking your parent all the way home will be one of the hardest, but it will be worth it.

Live each day with no regrets,

Rayna Neises, ACC
Regret-free Living Coach
www.ASeasonofCaring.com, www.NoRegrets-book.com

KYLE SPYRIDES

"Decide your destiny."

If a T-Shirt Could Talk...

About Me

Soul Gazing Photography - "Soul Gazing Photography helps remarkable business owners to create the next level of trust required to verify their services as quality and the only solution to go with, in their customers mind. We achieve this target by evoking movement in the hearts and souls of your ideal clients through creating a visual story that elevates your brand. This inspires those ideal clients to take action. The first impression we have on people has changed remarkably from physical to Digital and Print so capturing the essence of your business's problem solving ability invited those ideal clients in to see how the business owners decide to visually represent themselves and what quality they stand for.

This creates a sense of urgency in your ideal client to reach out and connect with you knowing through visual trust (seeing is believing) that you help facilitate their dreams in the mission and journey they're venturing on." Decide Your Destiny - "Decide Your Destiny is a spiritual evolution movement. The Philosophy and Action Steps of how to take more authority over your own (not owned) life and Design a Destiny that you desire has been cultivated from the Transformative Memoir - 'Decide Your Destiny'. This movement encapsulates a Network of 'Destiny Deciders' who launch their life into the direction they want to take it in everyday utilising the lessons shared on the DYD university. The core essence of Decide Your Destiny is to extract the heart and soul within so that we can live in alignment with the mission we came here to serve. The vision is of a better future where we simultaneously extract more humanity in each one of us prompting us to share in greater connection and spiritual elevation of our humanity. 'Decide Your Destiny' is more than just pretty words. They are the foundation of a philosophy that has seen Kyle through multiple 'Phoenix Rising' moments in his life. Kyle is the custodian of this philosophy from his grandfather who is the happiest man he has met. A man who smiled all the way to his last heartbeat at 90 years of age, it has become Kyle's mission to get this philosophy into the hands, hearts and souls of as many people as possible on this planet.

This movement is for those in the community that are looking to repair the fracturing of society, accelerated discrimination, mental health crisis and social disconnection rife on this Planet in our modern era. The light, the spark, the essence within and the pursuit of each being pursuing their most desired, spiritually defined destiny and be spark that lights the flame of renaissance period where we collectively build on the character of our soul and the excellence of potential in our hearts. A common ground to grow from rather than a 'anti' this 'anti' that dense discriminatory labelling mechanism are the aspects Kyle likes to connect with most to bring more energy, vibrancy and opportunity to the Common Good on Earth."

If a T-Shirt Could Talk...

From Kyle Spyriders' Interview
(Episode #138)

STACY JOHNSTON: "So Kyle, when you look at this path that you've taken from this young boy taking pictures and being a photographer now jumping off to be interactive, and do just like your grandfather asked you to do. Involving the community, and help our kids grow up and portray this life of service. If this was your chance and the world was your stage, what would your one line statement be? What could we print on your t-shirt?"

KYLE SPYRIDES: "Well again, it is something taken from my grandparents, because they were so inspirational. And you know, for years and years, I spent about 10 years with them. I mean, I was kicked out onto the streets when I was 14. And they were the people that I could go to; the only people that I knew to go to. I would go into their room every morning every night to chat to them to just learn from them and gain wisdom and absorb everything. They would be a little bit more removed than parents, because they were grandparents and they would observe and they'd ask questions. One thing my grandfather said, one summer's day, with the sun coming in kissing the side of his face, he just turned to me with this boyish charm and he just said, "decide your destiny." He said, decide your destiny, Kyle. Make sure whatever you do in your life, that you decide your destiny. I've taken that on, I haven't printed it on the shirt just yet, but that's the title of my book that I'm in the editing process of and that's the message that I'm taking through my life. I do a 'decide your destiny' blog every day and I make sure every day that I'm taking those words on in my own life. And I think it's really important, really powerful. Now I don't know why he had that boyish charm. Maybe he just uncovered some wisdom that he just thought, 'this will be great to impart on this youngster.' But in my youth, I didn't have clear direction of where I wanted to go, like many people. And once you do get that clear direction, you find your purpose. You identify the hero you want to be in your world for your family and for your community life just comes like a laptop for you. It's just magical. So 'decide your destiny' would be the phrase I would say."

STACY JOHNSTON: "I think that is absolutely beautiful. I think that's a training, right? That's a class in a day. That's a bumper sticker. It's a life statement, because so many people don't believe they have any decisions. I just have to get up and go through the flow and turn out to be this thing. You actually get a decision in it. You do get to decide a lot of it. Beautiful, beautiful sentiment."

If a T-Shirt Could Talk...

Dear Reader:

Two months out of school I was heading towards making my own legacy when my life was suddenly intercepted. I was put into an induced coma and my family were told that I would not wake up. I did wake up with a 3cm bug eating a hole into my heart. I had options. Two options. Go into the operating table and have a vital piece of my heart chopped off and replaced with a metal instrument forever changing the quality of my life. The second option was brought forward by my stepfather (a well rounded Chiropractor); The Alkaline Diet, something I had no prior knowledge of. I trusted the man and with my stepfather we did a juice fast for six weeks and drove the bug out of my body in three.

Twelve months later after successfully and naturally healing my heart I decided to have open heart surgery to repair any damage to my valve. I had options and I made choices. My life was forever impaired however I had the personal authority and responsibility to decide what direction the rest of my life would take. The question that has been stirring inside me is; Do the children of today have the same freedom of choice? Is life valuable to others? How do we help them to reign in power back within themselves? Assist them with life skills and how to keep those perishable skills sharp and ready for implementation in their lives and day to day challenges? Inspire them to become the authority over their lives and Decide their Destiny. Know thyself. Investigate what holds true within your heart and soul. The more attention and intention we bring to the integrity of these vital elements of our being evolves us from any attachments to the physical. This creates space for us to assume our own expression and creative discovery of what we are doing here in this time in history and what exciting and valuable aspects we are bringing here. We can then begin our true Journey. In Australia, 1 in 5 people are on psychiatric drugs for a huge range of so-called mental conditions. Firstly we can acknowledge how certain outlets in our world turn up the pressure in our lives and when our environment is heavily polluted by toxic rhetoric, divisive dialogue and fear porn that the most fantastic of writers could never have thought up is going to really stretch our mental capacity. Being raised by my grandparents it is very evident that their environment and grassroots culture gave them skill sets to face the most seemingly abominable force standing upright, shoulders back and proud.

Resilience, crisis-management, mental resource allocation and powerful visualisation when the picture doesn't look so pretty before you, make no mistake are perishable skills. You only attain them through hard and rewarding work, through life experience, through moving out of the crippling victimhood mindset and to whole-hearted ownership. Work on the development of these skills, let your progress and development do the speaking. Turn down the noises of people labelling you. They label because they can't comprehend, they are at a loss, in that very moment they are attacking you they are embodying that vile nature within themselves, they had to allocate and expend their energy into that toxic examination. Don't jump straight to the emotional reaction. Raise your awareness and see the reality of the situation. Just because they don't make sense of you or the work you are doing does not mean you can't make sense of it. It actually makes it even more yours to own. Own your space, own your mission, own your cause, and discard their toxic waste they splatter at you. Ask, is it constructive? Can I use it towards my mission? If not, hit the trash bin. Generally in my experience if they want to say you are wrong or not have to listen to you they label you crazy. They use the phobia of mental health because of your stance on something they label you crazy to cut off any communication. It's vile. A great response is: "Mind your own business, leave me alone." For a less abrasive response; "Oh hmm interesting, is that so." —Your response when you don't agree with someone and you wish to avoid confrontation and would like the communication to slowly fade away. The more you show your cards the more you are playing their game. You don't have to prove or convince anybody of anything but if they have questions feel free to communicate. Giving away freedoms, personal authority, responsibility and ownership is only going to multiply the issues we have as a society.

The more strength, fortitude, grit, resilience and faith we foster in our heart and soul despite how daunting the storm looks outside is the only way we put ourselves into a position of solving the problems generations on this planet will have to face. I am not sure apart from taking care of yourself and your family of a greater calling than to make this planet better for all not worse for the many to be better for the few. You make it better by first making your relationship with it better, you make existence better by first making your existence better, you make life matter by first making your life matter. Decide Your Destiny community focuses on giving you the skills required and platform to decide to live each heartbeat with high ethics achieving your greatest potential, purpose and vision resulting in you becoming joyously excited for each new heartbeat. You can sign up

NIGEL HARVEY

"Fightin' on faith!"

If a T-Shirt Could Talk...

About Me/Contact Me

Phone: 575-650-0337
Email: Bullfightin_nige@yahoo.com
Address: P.O.BOX 2515 Kirtland, NM 87417

Wisdom of Heroes

From Nigel Harvey's Interview
(Episode #157)

STACY JOHNSTON: "And so as you take this place as a recognized hero in the lives of so many people, if this is your opportunity to share your statement and your superhero mantra with the world Nigel, what's your statement? What does your t-shirt say?"

NIGEL HARVEY: "I'm actually coming out with some t-shirts here pretty soon and actually I got this really official for myself. It's the slogan that I've always used for the past 15, well ever since I started fighting bulls. It's been 'Fighting on Faith.' I've always come to that because I grew up with the traditional and also with the Lord inside of my house. I grew up with the teaching in the house, so I always put it back on 'Fighting on Faith.' Whatever you're going to come to in life, you know, you're going to come to some challenges and in one day, you're going to have to realize that faith is the only thing that's going to get you through the challenges. I've been all over the place and I've had a lot of adversity face me, but I've always thought, you know, God is always on my side. God put me on this path for a reason. God put me here to save a life, to be there for other people, to take the hard hits for the people, to sacrifice myself. Whether it be in the rodeo arena or outside the rodeo arena, I've always left the decisions I have to make within that quick instant up to God. And so I really believe in fighting for our faith. Pretty soon here you're going to see some great gear coming out from myself, which is really cool. It's gonna be 'Fighting on Faith' and I can't wait."

STACY JOHNSTON: "I can't wait! You know you're gonna have to share it with us, right? I want to own some of that for myself. Nigel, I just want to thank you. As we get ready to wrap up today I really heartfelt want to thank you. Thank you for just being a presence in my life, for the gift of your friendship that you've given to our family, to my children, for the people you save, for the lives you touch. I'm grateful to you and I'm just so honored that you're here with us today. I can't think of a better way to close this out than to give you the stage for sixty seconds. What's your closing comment, Nigel? Rather, what is it you want to make sure that the people hear?"

Dear Reader:

Love what you do. Take the time to realize that God has you on a path. It doesn't matter who you are, what you're doing, what kind of adversity you're facing right now. God has you on this path for a reason. And I always say, that small prayer, like my momma always said, your prayer the size of a mustard seed can move a mountain. I want everybody else to know out there, pray. It doesn't matter who you are, where you are, what kind of prayer you say, or what your beliefs are. Just pray. Just take that time to be thankful and grateful for who you are in this life. And continue to drive, continue to train your mind, your body and your soul to be a lot stronger for tomorrow.

If a T-Shirt Could Talk...

MARYBESS JOHNSON

"N.O.W. Not Over With"

If a T-Shirt Could Talk...

About Me

While continuing her own journey of self-growth, Mary Bess left retirement in 2016 to join the Maxwell Leadership Certified Team with the single thought of helping others grow and of fulfilling God's purpose for her own life. Whether serving the Global Maxwell Team, her clients or offering humorous wisdom to her 7 grandchildren, entrepreneur, wife, mother and dedicated community volunteer, Mary Bess has been helping individuals and organizations improve for decades. She serves as a Peer Teaching Partner and Team Leader on Maxwell Leadership's Connections Branch of The President's Advisory Council. Her company, Leadership Solutions N.O.W., LLC, provides leadership & personal development to individuals, businesses and organizations through coaching, training, speaking and DISC behavioral analysis. She and her husband Chris are active in Pendleton United Methodist Church and also reside in Pendleton.

Mary Bess Johnson
Leadership Solutions N.O.W., LLC
www.marybessjohnson.com
cmbj90@gmail.com
www.linkedin.com/in/marybessjohnson
803-424-7353

Wisdom of Heroes

From MaryBess Johnson's Interview
(Episode #158)

STACY JOHNSTON: "As you look at those things. At what you know, the path you've traveled, and the person that you've come to be, and you have a moment. This is your time to make your statement to the world. What does your t-shirt say, Mary Bess? What's your statement?"

MARYBESS JOHNSTON: "Stacy and Boyd, I had in January when I was deciding on my word for the year, you know, which we so often do every year. But now this word is going to be mine for my life. I won't be changing it I do not think. But in January, God said, Okay, girl I've got a word for you. It's NOW. So I wrote it down. And I looked at it, and I went, oh my goodness, Not Over With. And I realized that had been my heart now for a couple of years, where in the last couple of years I have gotten to the point of feeling so just so real and so authentic and just knowing who I am and whose I am and being okay with all of that. And knowing that I want to live a life of significance. And to have an impact, until I take my last breath. So, it's not over with. You can apply that to almost, really, to anything you can you can say it's just not over with. I'm not done yet. There's still more, there's still more. God can use me in different ways. And we never know how we are influencing someone. I saw it firsthand, even with my sister, the day of her memorial service when so many of her former players got up and spoke. I saw it with my Dad too in '85 when he passed away. I realized then people got up and said things about him. So really, my whole family really influenced me. But I'm not over with. Now is the word. I'm not over with, not over with."

STACY JOHNSTON: "And, again, I've been so impressed, as we've done these interviews, and we've talked to people, the stories behind what their statement would be are so beautiful. Thank you so much for the time you've taken with us. Thank you for sharing with us. We are so grateful, as we close out today. We just hope that you have enjoyed the show that you've learned, and you've listened and accepted the gold offered to us by Mary Bess today, and that you were inspired and you recognize the impact and what love for people can be about. I think the most appropriate way we can close out today is in the words of Mary Bess Johnson. NOW. It is not over with."

Dear Reader:

Closing Statement: It is never too late to live a life of significance.

If a T-Shirt Could Talk...

KURTIS CROSS

"Don't quit!"

If a T-Shirt Could Talk...

About Me

Kurtis Cross began as a "basement DJ" with aspirations of building a DJ business. At the age of 13, he borrowed $100 from his grandfather to purchase stereo equipment from a local dealer. From there, his dream was born. On September 6, 1986 he completed his first event... a fashion show at a local church. This was just the beginning.

His parents split when he was just nine years old. As his mother was his primary caregiver, the family struggled to make ends meet. Through the years, moving from apartment to apartment, Kurtis & his sister were raised by a mother who made sure that solid values and a Catholic Church upbringing were a part of the family DNA. Kurtis' high school (Montgomery Blair High School) and principal Phil Gainous were a solid source of support for Kurtis, making sure that he had a foundation for success.

As the years went on, Kurtis found himself as the DJ for more and more events. His grandmother's "Never Quit" mantra stuck with him and at every turn, Kurtis looked to increase his success by finding new clients, servicing his existing clients and exploring new areas of opportunity. One event at a time, slowly but surely, the business grew. Along the way, Kurtis has had many mentors... be it family, friends or strangers that he has come across. As Kurtis soaked up their wisdom, he learned valuable lessons about life, business & the world. Keeping in mind that all lessons are not learned conventionally, Kurtis navigated his way with the support of others. Some lessons and philosophies were learned through trial & error, but these were lessons learned nonetheless.

Today, Kurtis enjoys the work of a 36 year career, having built his company into a full scale DJ service with professional DJ talent for all events, lighting, sound, photo booths and more. Kurtis is also a wedding officiant and motivational speaker. Kurtis resume' includes producing events in more than half of the United States, one former U.S. president, the NBA, several television shows, education institutions, multiple NCAA athletic programs, the Federal Government and literally thousands of businesses and clients. Kurtis also enjoys being behind the mic as the in-arena announcer, play by play announcer and color commentator for 10 sports. You may have even heard his voice on any number of voiceover efforts, live sports broadcasts, etc. He is the producer of a handful of podcasts, including "Take A T-O With Turner & O'Neill", "Cross Talk: The Kurtis & Paula Show", "Conversations With Kurtis" & others. Kurtis is a native of Washington, DC and lives in the DC suburbs with his family... Paula his wife, and his children Chelsie & Adam.

kurtis@kurtiscross.com
www.kurtiscross.com | www.mapdja.com
301-942-4500 (Office)
Social | Instagram, Twitter & Facebook @djkurtiscross or @mapdja

If a T-Shirt Could Talk...

From Kurtis Cross' Interview
(Episode #159)

STACY JOHNSTON: "Kurtis in this conversation I've heard amazing things. I've heard about your heroes, I've heard about your family, I've heard about the man that paid for your college. I've heard strength, I've heard follow your dreams, I've heard serve yourself. Oh man, I've heard a love for Jesus Christ, all this knowledge, all this wisdom. And thank you for sharing your hero with us. But let's reverse the roles for a minute. And let's let you recognize, Kurtis, that you are in fact someone's hero. And I hope that you take that and recognize the impact that you've had on the people that you talk to; even if you don't realize it when you touch them. So with your hero cape in place, with this being your moment and your opportunity. Kurtis, what's your one word for the world? What does your t-shirt of wisdom say?"

KURTIS CROSS: "My t-shirt of wisdom? Wow. You know, a very good podcast, of course. And knowing this question would come up, I figured I would have something to say, something that sticks with me. What does that t-shirt look like? It looks like a 13 year old boy who borrowed $100 from his grandfather to start his business. It continues on with a young man who didn't know his place in this world. It continues on with a young man who went through the ups and downs of business. And who had to refer back to some of the lessons he learned to become a better business person. It goes back to a young man who didn't know how to be the right kind of leader to his staff. I've coached high school and college women's basketball and it continues with me struggling to find out what kind of coach I can be. But one of the things that's super important to me, one of the things that should go on my t-shirt would be us going back to that line; to get to something, we've got to go through something. And what are you willing to go through? What are you willing to do? What do you want to do to achieve your success, I would guess it would be a line that I put on a t-shirt that is not uncommon to anyone. And it would be "Don't Quit." I had so many opportunities where I could have thrown in the towel. And I could have quit what I was doing that I could have given up on what I was doing. When my parents broke up, I can look back to that, when I saw my mother crying because my dad left her I could have given up at that point, I could have seen her give up. But she didn't give up. And so, to persevere and to not quit, to always give your best and to know that if you quit, then you've stopped this effort of yours before you got to see its success. You know, success looks so different for so many people. But you know, I've heard this said before that, at some point, to achieve your success, you've got to step outside of your comfort zone, you've got to take a leap of faith. And when you take that leap, your parachute might not open right away. And you're going to take some bumps and bruises along the way. There will be forks in the road, there's going to be some hurt, there's going to be some pain, but you must endure that pain and overcome that pain to recognize what your goals are, and to reach that success. So my t-shirt would say 'Don't quit.' You don't quit when it gets tough. You quit when the goal and the task is complete. That's what I would want my shirt to say."

STACY JOHNSTON: "I think that's a beautiful statement. Kurtis, thank you for sharing that. And you can hear the passion in your voice. And it makes such a difference. People can talk and there's so much verbiage out there right now. And there's so much chatter out there right now. But there's not a lot of passion behind the chatter. I appreciate the passion that you bring to your words, and the passion that you bring to your story and to our listeners. So thank you so much for your time today. Thank you for your wisdom, and thank you for your transparency. I can't think of a better way to close; to get to something, we've got to go through something so just don't quit!"

If a T-Shirt Could Talk...
Dear Reader:

Closing Statement: I appreciate the opportunity to speak with your audience today. I hope your listeners have got a little something out of what I've said. Again, I like your podcast; I know there are a lot of messages to your podcast, I thank you for allowing me this space to bring my message to your listeners. If one person hears what I have to say, it makes a difference to them, this time was very worth it.

DWAN BENT TWYFORD

"The truth is in the red letters."

If a T-Shirt Could Talk...

About Me/Contact Me

Cellphone: 303-870-9034
Email: dwanbenttwyford@gmail.com
Website: Dwanderful.com
The Most Dwanderful Real Estate Podcast Ever
Address: 3804 Gunn Hwy d, Tampa, FL 33618

Social Media
facebook.com/Dwanderful
instagram.com/Dwanderful/
youtube.com/Dwan%5C+Bent%5C-Twyford%5C

From Dwan Ben Twyford's Interview
(Episode #165)

STACY JOHNSTON:"Okay, so I'm going to ask you, if this was your moment and the world was your stage. When you take that platform and don that cape, underneath what does your t-shirt say, Dwan? What is your one line statement to the world?"

DWAN BENT TWYFORD: "Well, I'm gonna give the sign off that I give on my podcast. I do my podcast, I have a sign off at the end of every show, and my sign off is; 'The Truth is in the Red Letters.'"

STACY JOHNSTON: "The truth is in the red letters. Explain that."

DWAN BENT TWYFORD: "Well, what do you think it means? The truth is in the red letters?"

STACY JOHNSTON: "What an interesting concept to think about."

DWAN BENT TWYFORD: "It is. And people email me all the time they go, what does that mean? What does that mean? I'm like, well, you go research it for a week and you can't figure it out, I'll tell you what it means."

STACY JOHNSTON: "You know, if I think if I think about what it means to me, the truth is in the red letter, my heart goes back to the Bible, because that's God's word. That's when He speaks. He speaks in red."

DWAN BENT TWYFORD: "That's exactly what it is. It's the words that Jesus spoke. They're all in red. And if you go back and you read everything Jesus said, Christian or not you go back and read everything Jesus said. The truth, the parables, everything we need to live a good life are in those red letters. That is exactly what it means. A lot of people, in fact, can't figure it out.. And then other people are like, Oh my gosh, those are the words of Jesus. I'm like, yes, they are. Because I read the Bible nine times through and everything in the red letters, there's not a single piece of bad advice in there. On their spouse or kids, how to run a business, how to treat people

If a T-Shirt Could Talk...

like every single thing, how to love yourself, love your neighbor, like every single thing that is good living advice for all people is in the red letters. STACY JOHNSTON: You know, that's good, Dwan. We've done 158 interviews. And we have 158 different quotes. I'm gonna say that one that's a phenomenal quote and that is mind candy itself and one day, I will have a shirt that says that. I want to be able to tell that story. That gave me shivers! That gave me chills! That is a great conversation piece."

DWAN BENT TWYFORD: "It is, it is. And you know, it's funny because I do a lot of speeches and presentations and stuff like that. And I always say, Hey, guys, listen, remember the truth is in the red letters. I've had so many people that go hey, I'm a pastor, and I've never heard anybody say that. I tell people, if you're gonna read the Bible, start with Matthew, Mark, Luke and John and I'm going to tell every single person from now on. Just read the red letters and see where it leads you. So I'm not really trying to boggle people. You believe in anything. You could be a Muslum, you could be anything. Read the red letters and see how you feel about it. Because everything in there is how we should live our best life."

CASSEY HOLLAND: "Those are the core values."

DWAN BENT TWYFORD: "Yeah, they're the core values of our best life and the best person, the best life is in the red letters. Before I started my podcast, I literally spent six months thinking I need the best sign off. It's got to be something powerful, something that people won't figure out. I prayed and prayed and prayed and prayed and one day I was reading the Bible. I was like oh my gosh, it's the red letters. That's what I'm going to tell people, the truth is in red letters. Boom! There it came, and now I've said it in 170 podcasts. It makes people have to think for a minute."

Wisdom of Heroes

Dear Reader:

I have been an avid real estate investor for over 30 years. I have been blessed to speak on stages with presidents, motivational trainers, celebrities, and more. When I made the decision to start a real estate investing podcast I remember thinking, "I need a killer sign-off like the famous newscasters use. Something that will cause people remember my show." If only it were that simple. I literally spent months writing down slogans and kept coming up empty. Nothing seemed to fit. Does that ever happen to you? You are trying to come up with a great idea for a business or a side hustle and nothing seems to fit. When nothing came to mind, I started to question if God wanted me to even start a podcast. Maybe I had "willed" it and it wasn't from God, maybe He has a different plan for me, was I acting on my own. It's funny how easily we can be convinced that we aren't hearing from God, isn't it? I had prayed, I was certain, and then suddenly I wasn't.

One afternoon, as I was pondering quitting before I had started, God impressed this great message on me and said, "Tell people that the truth is in the red letters." BOOM! I had my awesome sign-off – The Truth Is in The Red Letters! I was now ready to roll out these shows, climb straight to #1, get a syndicated podcast and be the #1 real estate investor in the world with people lining up to hear from me…lol. Does anyone else find that your timeline and God's timeline don't match? Happens to me all the time. I did start my podcast and it did climb in rankings, very slowly. After listening to other shows, I felt it was time to increase my shows from one a week to two a week. I distinctly heard God tell me to include a Bible study and tell people all the goodness He has in store for them and I remember saying, "Absolutely not!"

"Talking" about God and "teaching" about God are two very different things. I can talk till the cows come home, quote verses, and tell you how to deal with your issues. To "teach" is a whole new thing and I "explained" to the Lord that He had the wrong person on this one…lol. Does God ever do that to you? Give you an opportunity to share His word and your first thought is: NO? I sat on it for a few days and God would

If a T-Shirt Could Talk...

not leave me alone. Very begrudgingly I agreed and asked God what He wanted me to talk about. I have to be honest; I was a wreck thinking about doing a Bible study in front of actual people. I didn't sleep, I was nauseous, and I barely ate for days. I have no skills; I'm a regular person; what would I say; and who would even listen!

    I got my nerve up one day, wrote out a few verses, studied them to be certain that I had a good understanding, recorded them and the next thing you know I'm walking people through communion, teaching the Lords Prayer and helping people get saved. Now, I look forward to my "Business by The Book" sessions. What excites me the most is when people reach out to me and ask me what my "red letters" comment means. BTW – Everything Jesus said is in RED letters.

God has a calling for each of us. I believe most of us ignore the whispers from God when He wants us to start something new. How many times have you talked yourself out of something and later realized that God did want you to do that thing?

    It is all based on fear. Fear of the unknown; fear of what others will think; fear of failure; or fear of success. We live much of our lives in the "fear zone" and for no other reason than we let the fear win. If each person who reads this decided to stopping being afraid, what could you accomplish? Could you step out in faith and find that amazing spouse that God has for you? Could you take that new job? Could you ask for that well-deserved raise? What could you do if fear was not part of the equation? You could move mountains.

    You might be thinking, "Dwan, that easy for you. You are not shy, you are a public figure, you are successful." Do you think I started this way? I was fired from most of my jobs in my 20's. At 30 years old, I found myself going through a divorce with an eight-month-old child. Was I afraid? YES, I was terrified. I had no job skills, no formal education, and no money. It truly was my "come to Jesus" moment. I believe most of us find ourselves in a "come to Jesus" moment at some point in our lives. Many of us take the easy path, well…because it is easy! What if you took the path least traveled? What if you stepped out in faith? What if you said YES to the next opportunity? What if you trusted God? Realized that He actually has a plan for your life and that it is so much greater than you can imagine. What would happen then? When I was unable to find a good job and decided to fix-up a house and sell it, it never occurred to me that I would be speaking to you now. I never imagined I would write three best-sellers or that I would speak on a stage in front of 5,000 people. I would have sworn to you that those things would never happen. I would have sworn that because those things were not in my plan. They were in God's plan for me.

> "For I know the plans I have for you," declares the LORD, "plans to proser you and not to harm you, plans to give you hope and a future."
> Jeremiah 29:11 (NIV)

What if we let God make our plans? I challenge you today to take action on at least one idea that you have been putting off. Start one side-hustle or business. Take one class. Do one thing that you know God has been putting on your heart? Will it work out the way you expect? Let's hope not…lol. What if it works out the way God expects?

If a T-Shirt Could Talk...

SERGIO GUTIERREZ

"BOLD"

If a T-Shirt Could Talk...

About Me

Who is he?

Sergio Gutierrez has used his performing arts career to heavily influence his practice of painting and creating a wide range of pieces in the styles of abstraction, conceptual art, new realism, and photo realism. Being a self taught artist picking up a brush in the beginning of 2011, Sergio's paintings, with their striking contrasts, colorful patterns, and exuberantly painted imagery, give the expression of his high positivity and passion for the arts in many different forms. Interested in painting portraits and nude themes, Sergio Gutierrez always conveys a sense of joy and generosity of spirit.

Sergiosfineart.com
Truly fine art.

Wisdom of Heroes

From Sergio Gutierrez's Interview
(Episode #168)

STACY JOHNSTON: "So I have another question for you. You said just a moment ago that we all have an opportunity to be someone else's hero every day just by showing up, so let's give you that moment, Sergio, and let's put you on a pedestal for just a second and don the cape and recognize that you in fact, stand as someone's hero. As you take that place as the hero and you put on the cape and you take that piece on the stage, what's your one liner, Sergio? What's your statement to the world? What does your t-shirt say?"

SERGIO GUTIERREZ: "It's funny you asked this because I'm currently reading Evan Carmichael's book Your One Word. And my one word is bold. You know, and I make every decision through that. I'm looking at my planner right now and it just has a huge hashtag that says 'Bold.' So that's what my shirt says. It's just my one word that I make every decision by because again, I just think a lot of people nowadays are a little weak minded. They expect things to come to them and I've just realized to love boldly, like make bold decisions, in whatever you're doing to live boldly. To be a bold hero for somebody. There's not one hero out there that is not bold. Not one. So every hero is bold. So that's my one word. That's what my t-shirt would say."

If a T-Shirt Could Talk...

Dear Reader:

Closing Statement: Going back to the self image thing, I think that's one of the biggest things nowadays, anybody listening who feels less than worthy or is looking on instagram and seeing people drive nice cars, nice houses, all that stuff isn't important. What is important is peace of mind, positive self image; do whatever it takes to cultivate that first, become your own hero before seeking out someone else. Thanks for listening, appreciate you listening, and know every single one of you were born for greatness.

KOBEN PUCKETT

"There is no QUIT!"

If a T-Shirt Could Talk...

About Me

Occupation
Event Promoter/host of a Professional Bull Riders Touring Pro stop.

Life status
Pursuing recovery from a spinal cord injury through health & exercise therapy.
Press On Foundation board member.

Location
Amarillo, Texas (I call Amarillo my home)

Mailing address
16801 Dowd Ln.
Canyon, Texas 79015

Email address
Koben@kobenpuckett.com

Wisdom of Heroes

From Koben Puckett's Interview
(Episode #177)

CASSEY HOLLAND: "Let's put you in the spotlight for a minute and own the fact that you are someone's hero. And if you had to put a one liner of advice to the world on a t-shirt, what would it be?"

KOBEN PUCKETT: "Oh, I'm wearing it right now. It says 'There's no quit.' That's what's on my t-shirt. 'There's no quit.' I could elaborate on that a little. You can just hear it, and see it if you follow my journey. There's no quit! You know, 12 years post injury. I still want more better. Is that the word? No, I still want to get better. I still want to experience greater things in life. I still want more independence. There's no quit. But there's something to be said about this community that helps me do this. I've learned that there's no quit on those you care about. There's no quit on your loved ones. Nobody can fill that gap. Only someone named Jesus Christ who fills my gap for me, because He never fails me. And I know that every human being out there has potential to fail me. Has my dad let me down before? Yeah. Has my mom? Yeah. Everyone I've been close to one time or another in my life. You will have something come up where you're a little disappointed in them in something. Nobody's perfect. But we can't let that identify or drive a wedge in the community because that causes separation. And when there's separation, then you're not as equipped to keep pressing on, to have that work ethic, to have that try. So, there's no quit on those we love. And there's grace that comes in. Because there's only One that's filling it all."

CASSEY HOLLAND: "I think Grace is so important. I mean, I personally have been given an incredible amount of grace. And that is one thing that I am strongly trying to get across to people is that nobody is perfect, just like you said and everybody deserves grace."

KOBEN PUCKETT: "Absolutely, absolutely."

CASSEY HOLLAND: "Thank you for sharing that."

STACY JOHNSTON: "Koben, that's beautiful. I love it. You know you are episode number 175 for us, interviews that we've done with people, and everybody's quote is different, not one of them has been a repeat. It's not the same words, it's not the same passion, it's not the same story. And they are beautiful. I've said from the beginning I want all the t-shirts. I want a t-shirt with every one of these quotes on it. But I want a little pocket on there so I can put the story in there. So you'll know you have to read the story about the quote because the stories behind them are so beautiful and they're so passionate and they're so real, and I thank you so much for sharing yours with us."

Dear Reader:

Thank you Stacy so much, thank you Cassey, I'm honored to get to be here and y'all that means a lot to me. Wisdom: don't be afraid to give someone encouragement. Fear again, gets in the way, you fear someone is going to get a big head? Nah. Character is there before it, encouragement is just going to make them more of who they are. So if they need to get better, they're trying hard in an area, stepping into it, give them some encouragement. Because it'll just help it go, it's what we're here for. It's what community is for, to encourage others. So let's see some more heroes out there, I love it, thank you.

If a T-Shirt Could Talk...

JESS BONASSO

"*Be the change you wish to see.*"

If a T-Shirt Could Talk...

About Me/Contact Me

The Self Care Goddess
Brave Life Catalyst & Self-Rescue Coach | Author | Speaker for the Worn Out Working Wonder Woman
Phone: 720-333-6796
Website: www.JessBonasso.com
Meetup: www.Meetup.com/TheSelfCareGoddessCollective

Follow me on Facebook, Twitter, YouTube, or LinkedIn

From Jess Bonasso's Interview
(Episode #181)

STACY JOHNSTON: "So Jess, at the risk of running out of time and having to cut this short, I'd love to get all of our time in. Let me ask you one more question. Let's turn the tables and let's put you on the pedestal and recognize that the light that you shine and what you do, you are probably more people's hero than you recognize. And so, own that and take that to heart and know that you are loved and cared for by probably more people than you can imagine. So, as you take that place as the hero and you stand there with a world as your stage, Jess, what's your one line statement to the world? Of all the words that are out there, what's your one liner to the world, friend? What does your t-shirt say?"

JESS BONASSO: "Be the change you wish to see in the world."

STACY JOHNSTON: "I love it."

JESS BONASSO: "Yeah, that's it. It's all about integrity. You know, when I made that proclamation with my ex-husband, that I am going to own my life from this moment forward. What that meant was I'm going to become the person that I want to be number one and also that I want to see in the world."

STACY JOHNSTON: "Right, so what a beautiful statement. Thank you for that. So Jess, I cannot tell you how much I appreciate your time today. Your wisdom, your knowledge, and again, the space that you provide for people to get better."

If a T-Shirt Could Talk...

Dear Reader:

On Being the Change You Wish to See in the World
Dearest one…

Have you ever had a moment in time where it seemed like you were standing on the top of the world but deep down inside you actually felt fraudulent, insecure & fearful? I know I sure have. In fact, during much of my late 20's & early 30's I was at a place in my life where I was experiencing uncomfortable feelings of both success & failure. On the outside looking in you'd think I was the epitome of success…I was making over 6 figures after having worked my way up the corporate ladder over a 13 year period. I was also in a high level IT management position where I was well-loved, well-recognized & well-respected. I was also deeply sought after for advice & wisdom about all things "database"-related & I was extremely proud of the fact that I'd put myself through college & had just completed my graduate degree.

I had a core group of close-knit friendships, family that I loved, a beautiful home & a car, the ability to travel to ecxiting places & a husband that I loved very much. Seemingly, it looked like everything was going grand in my life but my physical, mental & emotional reality was something altogether different! You see…I was struggling with chronic stress, anxiety, depression. I felt worn out & exhausted most of the time. I was 40 lbs overweight. I was short-tempered, angry & irritable a LOT. I was operating from a negative & toxic mindset. I had chronic low back pain & degeneration of the spine so bad I was considering surgery. I felt insecure & unsure of myself. I felt lost & without direction. I felt stuck, hopeless & unsupported. And the worst part…I hated myself for feeling like a complete fraud, insecure & for being the toxic person I had become. In fact, it wasn't until I lost a dear friendship due to my toxicity that I finally woke me up & became aware of how toxic I'd become. When that friendship crumbled, my world crumbled with it & I finally woke up to just how unhappy & miserable I actually was.

I also realized that HUMAN ANIMAL (fight, flight, freeze or

fawn) & HUMAN EGO (unconscious self-sabotage) were running the show for me & it finally became clear how much of a victim I'd become to life. I vowed from that moment forward to take back responsibility for my life & to do whatever it would take to turn things around. Fast forward to today…After making that vow to turn my life around, I left the corporate world in 2006 & became a self-rescue coach, author & speaker which has been my profession ever since & is where I've been fortunate enough to help thousands of women (and lots of men too!) learn how to master the art of self-rescue. But you see… In order for me to turn things around & take back responsibility for my life, I had to first identify & then become the change I wished to see in the world. Why? Because my external world was a reflection or a mirror for something that was missing or not working inside of me. For example, consider the following…If you're attracting negativity, you are likely practicing negativity. If you're attracting positivity, you are practicing positivity. In essence…what you focus on (and practice) grows & that's what I was doing. I was focusing & spending all of my time & energy on what I didn't want & not enough time on what I DID want! And in learning how to consciously co-create my reality, I stumbled across a powerful way to become my own hero. At the end of the day, what I've come to realize is that any suffering I've been through is actually a beautiful sacred gift that I co-created into my reality to wake me up & teach me deep lessons & wisdom about what I do & do not want in my life. And, in order for me to become my very own hero, I knew that I would need to identify with & practice alignment to a higher, wiser, braver version of myself…What I now call today the Self Care Goddess! You see… The Self Care Goddess was born after I decided to leave the corporate world in 2006.

Basically, she is the inner hero that I've been practicing alignment to since I left that soul-sucking corporate career. In fact, the core values & energy I envisioned her to have is what I've basically built my entire life & business around ever since making the decision to leave & start my own business! How so? Because every day I practice being a living embodiment of her core values & energy & although I still stumble & bumble plenty, I've also learned a lot about myself along the way, who I am & what I now

If a T-Shirt Could Talk...

stand for. In fact, she is the one represents the more conscious, HUMAN SPIRIT side of my experience with qualities such as: CONSCIOUSNESS, SELF-LOVE, SELF-CARE, FORGIVENESS, JOY, COMPASSION, EMPATHY, INTEGRITY, TRUST, TRUTH, HONESTY, EQUALITY, GROWTH, GRATITUDE, COURAGE, COLLABORATION, COMMUNITY, CONNECTION, COMMUNICATION, HEALTH STRENGTH, PASSION, HEALING, RESPECT, AUTHENTICITY, VULNERABILITY, CREATIVITY, ROMANCE, INTIMACY, WHOLENESS, and GRACE.

The good news? The more I practice alignment to her core values & energy, the more courageous, authentic & whole I've become. And this is what I believe it means to become brave...Ultimately, it's to become the change we wish to see in the world. Consider this...If I hadn't been through hell in my 20's & 30's I never would've woken up & discovered what REALLY mattered in my life. I also wouldn't have learned how to find all the gratitude, growth & grace in literally EVERYTHING that has come my way over the years. In fact, I can say beyond a shadow of a doubt & with certainty that every single ounce of my pain & suffering has ultimately led me to more love & joy than ever before because I'm BEING the change I wish to see in the world. So there you have it...If you don't like your life, simply identify what a higher, wiser, braver of yourself would look & act like & then go out & practice being that person...Every. Single. Day. Who would that higher, hero version of yourself be? Take a moment to consider this. And as you practice alignment to this higher, wiser, braver version of yourself be sure to look for gratitude, growth & grace in everything that comes your way so that you can live, love, & lead from a place of courage, authenticity & wholeness. Isn't it time to become the change you wish to see in the world? In love, light & gratitude...

VANESSA NOEMI

"You are your own medicine."

If a T-Shirt Could Talk...

About Me

Vanessa Noemi Parrado is a Homeopath, Reiki Master, Intuitive, and Women's Health Coach with 25 years of professional experience in natural healing. Her interest in natural medicine started in her childhood and at 18 years of age, she chose alternative medicine for life. She trained as a massage therapist first, then as a homeopath, and energy healer, and has alsoexplored all kinds of somatic practices for health over a period of 20 years. Vanessa has studied with some of the world's most appraised homeopaths like Jeremy Sherr; Alize Timmerman and Divya Chabbra. She has been teaching homeopathy in the Transformational School of Homeopathy in Helsinki, Finland since 2008. Vanessa has worked with thousands of clients worldwide. She currently specializes in hormone health and fertility issues.

Her mission is to raise awareness of the side effects of harmful chemicals in the household and the side effects of birth control and other prescription drugs. Educating mothers on the safety and efficiency of natural medicine as well as sharing her love for essential oils and chemical-free living are her passions. She is a brand partner with the biggest essential oil company in the world and leads a community of 600 women in 5 different countries. Vanessa runs a successful online practice and coaching business and is working on launching a homeopathic online course for families. She is also a published co-author of the Amazon best-seller 'Caged no more.'

Website: vanessanoemi.squarespace.com
Instagram: @vanessaenesencia
Facebook: www.facebook.com/vanessanoemi007

Wisdom of Heroes

From Vanessa Noemi's Interview
(Episode #186)

STACY JOHNSTON: "Ok, we are going to switch tracks on you for just a minute and we are going to ask you to take a platform, put on the cape, and recognize that you, Vanessa, are probably more people's hero in a day than you know. By the love you put out, by the space you provide, by the healing you help people find. Just by that light that you shine, you in fact, are more people's hero than you know. So, thank you from all of us for providing that light for us to see and those shoulders for us to stand on."

VANESSA NOEMI: "Thank you, Stacy, thank you so much. And thanks for having me. It's always a pleasure talking to you."

STACY JOHNSTON: "The same. I love it. It is light for me, to get to have conversations with you! So with your crown on, with your cape firmly tied in place. This is your moment and the world is your stage. What's your one liner to the world, Vanessa? What does your t-shirt say?"

VANESSA NOEMI: "I would say, 'You are your own medicine.' I think that's the thing that sums up what we've been talking about, you know, we have whatever we need inside of us to heal ourselves; whatever the problem is. So I will go with that. You are your own medicine."

STACY JOHNSTON:" I love it. I love it. One of the greatest things I've learned from this podcast is the wisdom of so many people from so many places around the world. With 185 interviews, we talk to these amazing people, and we have these conversations. When it comes down to this statement. What's your one liner to the world? We have 185 different quotes. No one has repeated themselves."

VANESSA NOEMI: "Wow! That's pretty amazing."
STACY JOHNSTON: "Isn't that cool? I mean as a couple more statements and I'll have a whole closet full of the best t-shirts ever. I have one for every day!"

If a T-Shirt Could Talk...

VANESSA NOEMI: "Yeah, well, how many days in a year? 350,000? So you keep going, girl!"

STACY JOHNSTON: "I'm halfway there. You're halfway there and I'm halfway there in the t-shirt wardrobe. But some of them have to go into shirts for wintertime, I think. But these statements carry so much power and the stories carry so much wisdom. It's just an honor in my life and we get to share that with so many people from so many places. I mean, look, you're joining us today from Finland. And you have this beautiful message and this beautiful light of healing. And that's universal. And that doesn't have a boundary or a border or a country. We all want that. We all want help. So thank you for what you provide for the world."

Wisdom of Heroes

Dear Reader:

Thank you so much for being part of this project and reading the inspiring stories that the Uncaped heroes podcast brings to the world regularly. I am eternally grateful to the hosts of Uncaped Heroes for giving me the opportunity to spread my message of hope. It is not very often that one finds himself reading the story that comes from a t-shirt. My t-shirt stated, 'You are your own medicine' and if my t-shirt could talk, it would tell youthe following:

1. The symptoms of the disease are not a curse, they are part of your body language. They are there to tell you that something is not ok, they are there to catch your attention and to let you know, that something needs to be done differently.

2. Your body is always trying to keep your vital organs intact, and it will produce symptoms in your body, mostly in the places where they are not lethal. If you keep ignoring the signals and fail to make the changes needed in time, the disease will keep moving forward and deeper into the system until it damages your tissues and organs.

3. What the symptoms are trying to tell you will be a very personal message that has a direct connection to your lifestyle, your diet, your thoughts, and your relationships. Only you can find the message, understand it and then make the change from the inside out. That is what true healing is about. A professional, of natural medicine, is only there to guide you and give you hints on where the problem is and what to do about it but in the end, it is you who heals.

4. Your health, your well-being, and your happiness are your responsibility. I know this can feel daunting, taking responsibility is such a scary thing sometimes but it is the only way to health and happiness.

We have been convinced that disease is just bad luck, genes, or whatever. We are taught that the problem comes from the outside and so does the solution. We are taught that we are hopeless and that we are depending

If a T-Shirt Could Talk...

on pills to cope with symptoms that cannot be cured. While there are situations when one may really need a drug to stay alive, diabetes type one is an example of this, and while viral infectious diseases that become epidemics are a fact of life, how much or how bad these diseases will affect us is directly linked to how healthy our immune system and body are. These germs are all over and they are constantly around us and even inside of us. They do not always make us sick, why not? Here is some food for thought. Why do we not get sick every single time there is flu going around? My message is a message of hope, a message to tell you that you are more powerful than you think. That you are not hopeless when it comes to disease and that even in the face of death, we can make choices that will either support our health & wellbeing or will contribute to disease. If right now, you are suffering from a debilitating chronic disease, please know, that there are options outside of prescription drugs. Listening to your body, paying attention to your diet, your emotions, and being mindful of your past can help. Healing emotional pain can make a huge difference in how much your disease will affect you on daily bases. There are wonderful professionals that can walk this journey with you. You are not alone. Your body is the most amazing, perfect vessel, created by God to his resemblance. Remember that, now and always. You are your own medicine. Do not let anyone tell you otherwise. Sending you lots of hope and love from Northern Europe.

Vanessa Noemi

PHOEBE LEONA

"Move with joy!"

If a T-Shirt Could Talk...

About Me

Phoebe is an author, dancer, yoga/meditation/movement teacher, and guide. It was after a year of extreme loss in 2013 when she found herself in the vast open space in between her old life and a new life, that she dove deeply into her practices and began her company. The nOMad Collective that guides seekers and curious souls through their own transitions and the spaces in between.

Throughout that time, Phoebe also developed her movement/somatic practice, Mvt109™ for students to fully embrace the freedom of moving in their bodies, transforming old and held patterns, and reclaiming the vibrations and stories they want to bring to life. Phoebe also finds joy in sharing her story to help others in their healing. You can learn more about Phoebe's story on her TEDx Talk, her podcast The Space in Between, muti-author book, Caged No More, and her most recently her solo book, Dear Radiant One.

Feel free to use anything from there. In addition to contact information:
Phoebe Leona
Websites: PhoebeLeona.com | thenomadcollective.org
Email: Phoebe@nOMadalwaysatOM.com

THANK YOU!

Wisdom of Heroes

From Pheobe Leona's Interview
(Episode #187)

STACY JOHNSTON: "So let's turn around and put the shoe on the other foot and have you take our hand and step on a pedestal and recognize that you are in fact, probably more people'e hero than you recognize in a day. Take that minute and allow that presence to know that you are loved and you are revered by all the people that you bring light to and that you help. That's what heroes are: the ordinary people that come alongside us and do extraordinary things for us in their life. So thank you for being that sort of people. You stand in place for that. With that in mind, and with that spotlight on you, and this is your moment. And you have all the words there are out there in this world to choose from. What's your one liner to share with the world? Phoebe what does your t-shirt say?"

PHOEBE LEONA: "I think I'm gonna have to go with, 'Move with joy.'"

STACY JOHNSTON: "I love it! That's perfect. I love it! You know we've done over 180 interviews and we have not had a repeat quote yet."

PHOEBE LEONA: "I love it!"

STACY JOHNSTON: "There is so much light and so much inspiration out there that we don't even have some that are the same. They're all inspiring. They're all cool. And they're all different. I love that so much!"

If a T-Shirt Could Talk...

Dear Reader:

I want to acknowledge both of you. Cassey we just met very briefly, and Stacy, you and I also just met very briefly but we have been linked together just recently the past couple months because we will be part of our multi-author book, Cage No More. I just want everyone to know that was primarily women sharing their stories of breaking free of societal constraints. But I want anyone listening, female, male, however you identify yourself, that anything is possible. Anything is possible, you own your story. Watch that it isn't what is happening to you, but that it is happening for.

JEANNIE LYNCH

"Stop apologizing for your magnificence!"

About Me

Jeannie Lynch is an Intuitive Energy Healer, Spirit Coach & Teacher as well a content creator on Youtube. Jeannie's Spiritual Coaching Business focuses on helping others navigate through difficult times by giving her clients the tools and resources to assist them along their healing journey. She works with her clients to identify and remove negative energy blocks, limiting belief's, unhealthy thoughts or patterns that are preventing them from living the life their soul intended.

Jeannie left her corporate job in finance after 25 years to move to Florida where she started her own coaching practice. After years of helping Women Business Owners start and market their own businesses, she made the brave decision to do that for herself. Her desire is to Change The World One Video/Podcast At A Time, and to help her clients to be the best expression of themselves.

Socal Media
Youtube: https://www.youtube.com/channel/UCI6an0nuVs2541ieyZ6u-E3w
Anchor: anchor.fm/s/102a7b2c/podcast/rss
Email: Jelila63@Gmail.com

Love & Light Jeannie

From Jeannie Lynch's Interview
(Episode #192)

STACY JOHNSTON: "Thank you so much for just recognizing those people around you, and for what you do, Jeannie. The space that you provide for people to come in and be in. So let's reverse the roles for just a minute. And let's put you up here on stage and recognize that you are probably more people's hero in a day than you recognize. So thank you for stepping up and coming alongside the people that you do and that shoulder and being that person to help them along the way. So, with your robe firmly attached, cape in place, as the hero, and all the words that are out there in the world, what's your one liner to the world? What's your t-shirt say?"

JEANNIE LYNCH: "I love that question. By the way, my t-shirt out to the world would be, 'Stop Apologizing for your Magnificence.' It's our divine birthright to be magnificent. That we are all born perfect. And then we get it all messed up in our head. So the people who were like, 'Oh, I'm sorry, you know, I'm like talking too loud.' And you know, I show up that way and we tend to lose our power as we go through life because we become an excuse for ourselves. Well, I didn't know that at the time. I was misguided or I married that guy. I had that mother. You know, these excuses show up. But the truth is, we're the only ones who get to control how and who and why we show up the way we do. So there's no apologizing for who we are. And so stepping into your magnificence, to me, was just accepting the fact that we're on this road to just to be imperfect but to be perfect, right?"

STACY JOHNSTON: "I love that. I love that! Yes. And I think I think you'll agree with me Jamie, one of the coolest things that we have gotten to experience in this whole thing is 180 plus interviews. And nobody has the same quote. They're not even close. Thank you for sharing that. Stop Apologizing for your Magnificence. Beautiful!"

If a T-Shirt Could Talk...

Dear Reader:

If you are reading this letter, I can only assume that you have been through some kind of life experience like me, that has led you to these pages at this exact moment in time. Maybe you've experienced a difficult challenge or a dark period of time in your life where it was hard to see the forest through the trees.

I've come to understand that those exact moments are the times that can either break-us or define-us. I've titled those moments in my life "By The Grace of God" I do believe that before Grace can come into your life there must first be the SPACE to feel it, Grace is something you need to ask for and you certainly need to be open to receive it.

I've also learned that in order for you to feel Grace you need to witness it, acknowledge it, appreciate it and most importantly be will to share your Grace with others. I share my Grace in my Spiritual Coaching Practice with the clients I serve, as well as by creating spiritual content for my on YouTube channel.

As a content creator and Intuitive Energy Healer/Teacher I love creating videos by doing guest interviews with other healers from around the globe and with people who have inspirational stories or spiritual modalities that want to share. My intention with my social media platforms is to inspire, educate and support others on their own spiritual journey.

In 2005 when I lost my only daughter in a tragic car accident I found myself wishing (searching) for guidance. I found so many beautiful paths, tools and energy healers to work with along my way but I also felt pulled in so many different directions.

Unable to find one place to go I decided to create one. I've spent the last 17 years creating spiritual content with the one intention to make spirituality accessible and easy to understand, as well as able to apply different spiritual principals into your own life.

Wisdom of Heroes

The Intuitive Mindset School with Jeannie Lynch on YouTube has 20 different playlist and over 365 videos that are out there to help you navigate your own spiritual awakening healing.

My promise to the spiritual community I serve is simple.
You will…
1) Be Safe
2) Learn & Expand
3) Heal
4) Laugh & Cry
5) Expand your Soul

If you have an offering that would be a great addition to my channel, please reach out to me I'm always interested in collaborating with other like-minded individuals. This year I'm focused on creating content for the following three playlist.

Teaching others How to Connect To Their Intuition.
Spiritual Stories Worth Sharing
Spiritual Modalities for a Spiritual Life.

I hope the stories and letters in this book have Graced your day. If you need any help or guidance to find your own way through The forest in your life please reach out to me on email @jelila63gmail.com.

Love & Light Jeannie :)

If a T-Shirt Could Talk...

CLAIR BRADSHAW

"You have everything inside of you."

About Me

Claire Bradshaw is a certified holistic life and business coach, meditation teacher, author and host of Becoming Whole podcast. She supports women from around the globe, both privately and in powerful group containers, to be the conscious creator of their own life. For the last 5+ years Claire has been guiding her clients to break-free from automatic living & burn out, and to step into the intentional, passionate and powerful life that's truly calling them. Claire uses a unique blend of ancient yogic philosophy & energy principles, along with scientifically proven coaching models and powerful questioning techniques to help her clients connect deeply with themselves and bring their gifts out into the world. Her work is grounded in her belief that the world needs more of us to reclaim our authentic power, purpose and passion and to express this, both for ourselves and for the future of humanity

Instagram:_clairebradshaw_
Website: claire-bradshaw.com
Podcast: Becoming Whole
Book: Caged No More

Wisdom of Heroes

From Clair Bradshaw's Interview
(Episode #193)

STACY JOHNSON: "Let's take it to our final question. Clair, let's switch roles for just a minute. Let's allow you to stand up on the pedestal with a hero cape on, and realize that you're probably more peoples hero than you recognize in a day. So thank you for being that light, and that vision of hope for so many people around you. Please don the cape and realize your own hero status to the world around you. And with that in mind, in that place where the world is your stage, of all the words to choose from, what is your one liner to the world? What does your tshirt say?"

CLAIR BRADSHAW: "What a beautiful question, thank you for asking it. My statement would be, 'You have everything you need inside of you.' Go inwards and discover, and then bring that out into the world."

If a T-Shirt Could Talk...

Dear Reader:

Closing Statement: "Thank you so much Stacy, and this has been a wonderful podcast. My offering to your audience is to stay true to yourself. To connect within yourself everyday, and know that there is a stock within you, there is a light within you. Every moment of every day you can reconnect to that place and the world that special gift that only you have. Bring more of you to the world."

JAMIE MARTIN

"Be couriosity, be courage, be compassion."

If a T-Shirt Could Talk...

About Me/Contact Me

Jamie Martin is a Life and Leadership Coach who is passionate about helping people who have been going so long they have lost themselves. Working with Jamie, her clients end up standing in their full power, even when they are doing the uncomfortable things they have always dreamed of doing. Her 17 years in technology as a Product Manager at companies like DoubleClick and Google taught her the value of bringing curiosity to her clients hidden needs. She's learned that often what we say we want goes deeper than surface level and may just be a workaround for our true desires. She's incorporated this concept into her work with clients to allow them to go deeper in order to expand and grow beyond their current perceptions of what is available in life. Pairing her years in technology and intensive coach certification gives Jamie a unique perspective into what it takes to make a significant transformation for her clients. Her clients consistently say that Jamie is able to cut through the noise and deliver immediate aha moments that result in a new passion for work and life. Jamie has been featured in Forbes, Medium and Ellevate on topics ranging from innovation to creating personal boundaries. She's also been a guest on "What Has My Attention" with John Biethan, Data Bytes by Women in Data and various other podcasts. And don't forget to sign up for the Reignite Your Brilliance Newsletter!

Jamie Martin, ACC—Life and Leadership Coach
Website: jamiemartincoaching.com
Instagram: @jamiemartincoaching
LinkedIn: https://www.linkedin.com/in/jamiemmartin

Wisdom of Heroes

From Jamie Marin's Interview
(Episode #195)

CASSEY HOLLAND: "So, in combination with the things that you've learned, and the things that you pass on, if you could put a one liner on a t-shirt as your message to the world, what would it say? And why?"

JAMIE MARTIN: "It would say: 'Be Curiosity, Be Courage, Be Compassion.' Curiosity is one of the gifts that I think we have let go of in our lives because we feel that we need to know every answer. Yet, curiosity is a gift of how we can start to see the beauty in life. Ask big and small questions that can actually spark more excitement. I look at my son and he's just so curious about the smallest little thing. When we can get back to being curious, not only do we get a deeper connection to ourselves, but we get deeper connections to other people because we're coming from a place of curiosity when we're interacting with others. Courage. Courage is one of these because you have to be courageous, in order to live a full, vibrant life because it takes courage to step out of your comfort zone. And in order to have that vibrant life and really get out of your comfort zone you need to do the scary thing and shake life up a little bit. That looks different for everybody. But courage is the thing that makes that happen. You can continue down the path you're on and have that status quo that feels really gray. I think that's a good kind of descriptor for it. It's just gray, not sharp where it's so black and you're depressed and it's not bright and shiny. But to step into the bright and shiny you have to sometimes go into the dark, so it takes courage to be willing to do both sides instead of staying in that center. And finally compassion. Compassion is one of these. I think we've really latched on to empathy a lot. When you hear it, it's all over the place. If you start to look at the definition of empathy versus compassion, empathy is where you are actually feeling into somebody else's experience, so much so that you may not be able to get out of it and be able to walk alongside. Whereas, compassion is seeing them, understanding where they're at, and still being able to say, I'm here, how can I help as I walk alongside you as you're going through this experience? And really, compassion is such a beautiful place to come from as a person, both from a business perspective, but also from a human perspective, like getting in that place of seeing that somebody is hurt and that they're in pain, and maybe they need that from us."

STACY JOHNSTON: "I love that!"

Wisdom of Heroes

Dear Reader:

Hello There! Go back in time with me for a minute. Rewind the clock to the day you were born. You were thrust into an unknown world where the only sound you recognized in the cacophony surrounding you was your mom and dad's voice. You opened your eyes and there was light, people and objects all around you. Everything was new and scary. That was the first day you chose to be curious and be courageous. Despite your fears, you grew. One day you learned to smile and laugh. You learned to sit. You learned to pull yourself up to a stand. Before you knew it, you were progressing from crawling to walking to full out running. Climbing everything in sight. You explored the world around you. You tasted everything - your fingers, toys, rocks and food. You dropped your food testing gravity. You created art with crayons and paint.

Each thing you learned, you had to be curious and be courageous. You had to challenge yourself to step out of the comfort of your mom's arms. You cried a lot. You struggled a lot. You got frustrated a lot. You kept exploring. You kept trying. You learned. You learned you have to hold your head up before you can sit up. You learned to walk before you ran. Everything took many, many tries. A lot of time being uncomfortable, but you did it. You learned. You grew. And when you got it, the smile and pride on your face lit up the whole house. You were born to be out of your comfort zone. To lean into curiosity and explore. To be courageous and try something new. Overtime, something changed. Your curiosity was dampened. What happened? Fear eclipsed courage. Fear took over. You learned that fear could protect you. Protect you from being hurt. This fear grew and grew. You learned to be fearful of what could happen. You became afraid of failure. You became afraid to be sad. You become afraid of crying from the struggle. You became afraid of being wrong. You became afraid of success. You became afraid of being in the limelight. You became afraid of being yourself. You started to protect yourself from what could be. You played it safe with your dreams, your heart and everything in between.

Think about it for a moment. What has fear stopped you from doing? Stopped you from dreaming? Stopped you from saying yes to

If a T-Shirt Could Talk...

a dream job that was challenging? Stopped you from speaking up in meetings? Stopped you from asking for support or help? Stopped you from loving someone else? Stopped you from loving yourself? You can allow this fear to hinder you. You'll continue to live your life exactly the way you have. Inside a nice little comfortable bubble. One that isn't that comfortable at all. One where you are drained from drama, lonely and simply unhappy. Or you can take what you were already born with, throw in some compassion for yourself and put it all to action right now. Take everything you learned as a baby: a little cry is ok, struggle is ok, failure is ok and being comforted, cheered on and supported is ok and allow yourself to take the first step outside of your comfort zone. The more steps you take the more you'll see yourself smiling along the journey. You'll laugh with the mistakes you make. You'll be proud of yourself. Imagine it for yourself. You have everything you need to jump into the unknown. You were born with curiosity and courage and compassion - you can practice compassion for yourself. You were born stepping out of your comfort zone. What will you create? What will you try? Who will you love? Be Curious. Be Courage. Be Compassion. Cheering you on as you take the first step,

ANNETTE MARIA

"There's no better time than Now!"

If a T-Shirt Could Talk...

About Me

Annette Maria is a Somatic Soul Coach, Intuitive Sound + Energy Healer, Author & Founder of Sanctuary Publishing. She supports burned out visionaries to return back to themselves with a holistic approach infusing the mind, body and soul. Annette believes in living alongside the dream to not lose yourself to all that you are building. She is an advocate for everybody learning how to cultivate inner safety & radical self-trust.

Email: hello@activationsbyannette.com
Facebook: facebook.com/annettemaria123
Instagram: instagram.com/its.annettemaria
Website: activationsbyannette.com
Insight Timer: insig.ht/annette.activator
Host of Sacred Dance Podcast

From Annette Maria's Interview
(Episode #198)

STACY JOHNSTON: "Okay, Annette. Let's switch the pedestal around for a minute. Let's change tactics and let's put you on the hero platform. Give you a moment to recognize that you are probably more people's hero in a day than you notice. Thank you for that, that hero that you provide for other people. That you can be that person that comes alongside and is that shoulder to stand on, or to stand beside. So thank you for that and thank you for what you do for the people around you."

ANNETTE MARIA: "Thank you, I received that wholeheartedly with a few tears running down my face. That was beautiful. Thank you very much."

STACY JOHNSTON: "You are very welcome, becauseI think we all want to live to make a difference. Right? We want it to matter in some way. And it does. So with that cape on and the world as your stage, what's your one liner, Annette? What does your t-shirt say? What's your one line segment of wisdom that you're going to share with the world?"

ANNETTE MARIA: "My one line statement is, 'There's no better time than now.' Just to feel widely expressed and who you are and what you are meant to do. Now is your time to rise into that."

STACY JOHNSTON: So there's no better time than now. Love it. Love it. That's beautiful. So if you had a chance to tell people around you that there's no better time than now, what would you say?"

ANNETTE MARIA: "Absolutely. We all have a gift, a purpose, a mission on this planet. And if you are feeling dormant, contracted like your light has been turned off in some form that you have been dimmed; know that you have the ability to reignite that and that your mission, your purpose in that moment is to reignite it. Not just for yourself but to shine it around for the others around you because we're all here for one another. And your time now is to rise up in how you are meant to be a service for yourself which then allows you to be of service to your family, the people closest to

If a T-Shirt Could Talk...

you and then that ripples out to the world. And you know, the world needs more joy, more light right now more than ever, and where are we going? What do we see? What do we want it to be more of? What do we want to see more of and how can we co create that amongst whatever is happening externally? How can we co create what we are desiring on this planet?

And now's your time to do that because I think that's really what has been taught to us that we don't really have time to waste. We don't know when a day may be the last or when something may happen. Honoring each day as the blessing that it is, and honoring yourself as a blessing that you are."

Dear Reader:

Thank you so much Stacy and Cassey, this was such a beautiful conversation. I would just love to leave the audience with even thinking that something is too late, you're perfectly on time. Even if you're feeling stuck and confused, that is where you're meant to be. Know that, keep stepping forward. We're being called to trust and just to take the steps forward. Break out of the shell that has been you previously, allow yourself to be reborn, transformed, because that is current energy that is holding us all. You have that choice within you, I invite you to know that you are never alone in the process. That is how I would like to leave your community today; share that nugget, that you are never alone and you are always deeply held in the same tangible realm of people around you, but also in the unseen realms. However you want to connect, God, grace, Spirit, you are always held in your life.

If a T-Shirt Could Talk...

MATHILDE ANGLADE

"You got this!"

If a T-Shirt Could Talk...

About Me

Mathilde Anglade is an actress & music performer, as well as a self-development guide and medicine woman. She lives a path of devotion to spirit through love, authenticity and freedom. For acting and music performances, connect with @mathilde_anglade on Instagram. For self development & medicine, connect with @mamamedicina on Instagram.

Phone: +61 413 648 112

From Mathilde Anglade's Interview
(Episode #199)

STACY JOHNSTON: "Let's turn the tables on you just a little bit and let's put you on the pedestal and let you recognize that in what you do and in who you are and in the light that you shine you probably stand as a hero to more people than you recognize. So, take that information and then own that for yourself. In that place where you stand as a hero and the world is your stange. Of all the words that there are out there, what does your t-shirt say? What's your one liner to the world?"

MATHILDE ANGLADE: "It would be, 'You got this!'"

STACY JOHNSTON: "'You got this.' I love that! Expand on it. Talk about it for just a minute."

MATHILDE ANGLADE: "I think I feel like in a lot of my friendships sometimes a lot of people come to me to talk and to share, to express and sometimes I see them as a reminder that everything is going to be okay that they have got this. It's a journey. We're going to unpack what they're feeling and then they can remember their power and like they've got this. They've got this. This craziest journey that life is. It's gonna be okay. Sometimes it's something very simple to hear you got this."

If a T-Shirt Could Talk...

Dear Reader:

I would like to say first, thank you so much Stacy and Cassie for creating this beautiful space and for having me. I'm sending blessings to you to, to your family, and to everyone who is listening. If anyone needs support, may they reach out. May everyone have a beautiful day full of kindness and love. And so it is.

TANA INSKEEP

HERO

"Everything is 'figureoutable'!"

If a T-Shirt Could Talk...

About Me/Contact Me

Tana Inskeep
Leadership and Mindset Coach l Speaker
Phone: 415-755-7499
Email: tanainskeepcoaching@gmail.com

Wisdom of Heroes

From Tana Inskeep's Interview
(Episode #207)

CASSEY HOLLAND: "So leading on into that, we will put the cape on you for a minute and let you sit in the spotlight and recognize that you are in fact more people's hero than you think. So thank you for that. I think you mentioned it a while ago, but if you had one liner to put on a t-shirt what would it say?"

TANA INSKEEP: "It would be, 'Everything is figure-outable.' And underneath that I would put this too shall pass, because I think it goes back to the feelings. I think we can get so overwhelmed by a moment and call it a bad day when it was just a bad moment. And to know that this suffering, this problem, it will pass. I've had so many dark times where I thought, get me out! Take me out of this place. Right. And recently around our community there's been a few teenage suicides, especially in men. And I just always wonder, like, what is it that I heard? You know, it's like literally the decisions made in 20 minutes. It gets so much despair, it compounds and then it's just done. But moments pass, a feeling passes, you know, the circumstances will pass. And I just love that because it gives me hope, especially in the dark times, because we do have dark times. But just to remind yourself of this too shall pass. This nervousness shall pass, my anxiety will pass, my fear will pass. And if it's not in this lifetime, we know, we know it's gonna pass."

STACY JOHNSTON: "I love that Tana, there's just so much hope in that right there. And I think that's one thing that people right now are just looking for right, those moments of hope, those places they can hang on to, that space where they can get better. It's okay over here to feel like that. There's just so much of it there and it's just beautiful to see."

CASSEY HOLLAND: "And realizing that you can't have one without the other. You know, you don't learn to appreciate the sunshine unless you are in the rain. Or vice versa. You know, you can't have one without the other. So you have to learn to appreciate them all."

If a T-Shirt Could Talk...

TANA INSKEEP: "Yes!. And to know that it won't last. To remind ourselves, it's like collecting evidence. I feel like because sometimes in a moment it can feel like it just dissolved. It's always gonna be this way, like COVID. Right? Like COVID will pass just like the bubonic plague and just like your storms that come in; hurricanes, the flooding, it does pass. It's like Who do I want to be in this moment? How can I anchor into hope right now and be calm and be the hero now in the midst of this dark place?"

STACY JOHNSTON: "It's so very true. It does pass. So many things we think when we were in the middle of it that it's not. This thing that has happened and this moment that I'm sitting in now defined my life and no it hasn't. It's just designing you. It really gives you what you need. Just designing you, that's all."

Dear Reader:

Closing Statement: I just want you to know that you have infinite worth and infinite value. It's okay if right now you don't believe it, but the truth is, it's not about what you bring to the table. It's not about your skills. It's not about your personality. It's about you being human and you being you. The sky is blue. And sometimes there's clouds that cover it, and we think the sky is black or gray, but that's not true. It's just covered, the sky is blue, the sky is always blue, it will never not be blue. That's like your worth. You will always be worthy. You will always be beloved. That is who you are. It doesn't matter, you can fight it, you can believe it, you can not believe it. But the fact is, you are worthy and you have worth, and you have infinite value because you were created by an invaluable God. He doesn't make junk. His fingerprints are all over you. You look at your fingerprints, there is only one of you. You are a masterpiece, whether you believe it or not. What I want to offer you is to start working to believe it. Look at that sky, it is always blue, always. Just like you, always worthy, just believe it. It doesn't matter how you've been treated, or what you think about yourself, or what you bring. No, you just are. You can feel anything, and still be worthy. You can feel shame, still be worthy. Feel disappointment, still be worthy. You just are. Now it's time to decide to step into value, to believe it, and to go shine.

If a T-Shirt Could Talk...

HOPE REGER

"Invest in hope!"

If a T-Shirt Could Talk...

About Me/Contact Me

You can connect with Hope here:
Website: grief2hopesupport.com
Facebook: facebook.com/hope.day.3975
Facebook: facebook.com/Grief2Hope2020
Instagram: instagram.com/grief2hope2020/
LinkedIn: linkedin.com/in/hope-reger

Wisdom of Heroes

From Hope Reger's Interview
(Episode #208)

STACY JOHNSTON: "Alright, let's take it from another spot, okay? Let's reverse the role. Let's take it around, turn it around and let's put you on the pedestal for a moment and recognize that you are probably more people's hero in a day than you know. The people that you bring hope to, the people that you shed light to, the people you go, 'look, there's a light at the end of the tunnel down here.' Thank you for being a hero to them. So with that cape firmly attached, on your platform girl, you're a superhero. What is your one line statement to the world. With all the words that are out there, what does your t-shirt say?"

HOPE REGER: "I'm gonna have to say, 'Invest in Hope.' Hope creates some strength and courage inside ourselves that we never knew existed; especially when we're grieving. So I would have to absolutely say invest in hope and know that there is a brighter side. It may be harder tomorrow, but the next day it may not be, and just keep living strong. So invest in hope, I think, would have to be on my T shirt, that's for sure!"

STACY JOHNSTON: "I love that. I just get chills. And I get this like 'wooo!' moment, you know? You just kind of want to holler! I get this rush of hope from it. Hope, I want to share with you, we've done over 200 podcasts now. We've done over 200 recordings from people from all over the world. And we've asked this very same question just to get that one liner of wisdom. And we have 200 absolutely different quotes. Nobody repeats themselves, they're not the same in nature. There were like 200 categories of help the world. It's the coolest thing. I have a power closet!"

HOPE REGER: "Yeah, you need to like put them in a book for a daily reminder."

STACY JOHNSTON: "You know, we're in the process of writing a book right now off this podcast, because, like I said, the quotes that we've gotten, the statements that we've gotten from people have so mutch power behind them, so much hope, there's so much encouragement that we're actually

If a T-Shirt Could Talk...

putting them together and we're going to put them out 50 at a time. It has just the t-shirt statements and the stories behind them. And the stories behind the stories are powerful. I love that. Beautiful. I can't wait!"

Wisdom of Heroes

Dear Reader:

Hello, my name is Hope Reger. I am the creator of Grief 2 Hope, a virtual peer grief support group I created in honor of my son, Justin who was murdered in 2016 at the age of 19. It has been my mission to create a community for individuals who are experiencing grief, a safe place to be their authenticate self while providing hope, positivity, and support along their journey. To let them know that having joy once again in life is achievable and they are worthy. My program meets on an ongoing rotational seven weeks that speaks to different topics each week.

G R I E F 2 Hope
Week 1—Introduction   Week 2—Gift of Time
Week 3—Receive Help   Week 4—Inspire
Week 5—Expectations   Week 6—Feel Everything
Week 7—2 Hope

Please visit my social media sites as well as my website for all details and my contact information. You do not have to do this grief journey alone "Invest in Hope."

Website: grief2hopesupport.com
Facebook: facebook.com/hope.day.3975
Facebook: facebook.com/Grief2Hope2020
Instagram: instagram.com/grief2hope2020/
LinkedIn: linkedin.com/in/hope-reger

If a T-Shirt Could Talk...

CALLIE KNAPP

"Be the role model!"

If a T-Shirt Could Talk...

About Me

It's been said that "Horses carry the wisdom of healing in their hearts and offer it to any humans who possess the humility to listen" (-author unknown).

My name is Callie Jo Knapp and I live in Moriarty, NM. I am a mother of two beautiful girls, ages 1 and 6, a wife to a Professional Bull Rider, and a Mental Health Therapist for the Pueblo of San Felipe. I grew up in a rodeo family and enjoy the western way of life. Horses have always been a part of my life and I truly value their God given gift to heal and transform our hearts and minds. I believe that there are certain skills learned best when interacting with, and responsible for, another living being.

I also believe that time spent outdoors is what the world needs more of. Today, I specialize in Equine Assisted Therapy, (using a horse as a therapeutic tool) to address mental health disorders such as, but not limited to, trauma, anxiety, depression, ADHD, grief, and so much more. I have found that with a hands-on, experiential approach, the skies the limit. There's something innate about connecting with animals and nature. Both personally and professionally, I am blessed with a daily opportunity to positively influence others. This is a chance for me to apply the skills that I have learned to my clients and to my own children, and to be a healthy role model to all. I believe that it's a choice to lead an intentional life, and this starts with self-reflection and self-help. Although I may often fall short, I believe in accountability, humility, respect, and genuine empathy. I believe in the power that we each have on one another and choose to have an affirmative impact.

Wisdom of Heroes

From Callie Knapp's Interview
(Episode #213)

STACY JOHNSON: "Let's turn these tables on you for just a second Ms. Cali and put you up on a pedestal for just a second, and let you just take a second to own the fact that you are probably more people's hero in a day than you recognize. I know your husband, and to those two beautiful girls you __. So own that, because we all have to find a place to be your own hero and to recognize you got this. Take that for just a moment, and in that place, Cali where you stand as that hero, if the world was your stage, all the words that there are out there, language that you speak, what is your one-liner to the world Ms. Cali? What does your tshirt say?"

CALLIE KNAPP: "Oh man, I , 'Be the role model.' You talked about language, and I think a lot of times that comes, our first thought is to take it in what we speak, body language and our actions. Not just in what we can say out loud but what we can show through our actions and our movements. The body language we speak as well, be the role model to others that you do have or would like to have in your own life. Role model for others and let those actions match up with your worth."

Closing Statement: "I really like what Cassey said, tying it all back to this conversation and that we can't control the decisions that other people make, but we do have our own choices. If you recognize that you need something to shift in your life, that you have the choice to create that change for yourself and those that you love and care about. If you do that self inventory at the same time, see who you can reach out to for help or guidance. Be forgiving of yourself and understanding, but at the same time don't settle for less. Challenge yourself each day, create that change in your life each day. We never stop growing, we shouldn't, or learning."

If a T-Shirt Could Talk...

Dear Reader:

As I take a moment to reflect on my life, I am recognizing how much a good role model means to me. Throughout the different seasons of my life, I have been fortunate to have people in my circle who have seen me through some of the most exciting and challenging (and everything in between) experiences. These role models have joined me in celebrating my successes and grieving my losses. The most impactful role models have counseled me without judgement and have shown me grace, dignity, forgiveness, kindness, and patience. From them I have learned about the importance of accountability, self-acceptance, a strong work ethic, and so much more. Some have come and gone with the season, and others have remained steadfast, but either way, each have impacted my life in a special way.

As a mother of two, I recognize more than ever, how crucial positive role models are. It is our responsibility to shape and mold our children. We are the ones who they look to for guidance, to show them how to lead a life of dignity. We are the ones who teach them how to recognize healthy influences so that when they go off into the world they know who to gravitate toward. Sadly, not all children will have this in their own homes and they will search to fill the void. And so, we have an opportunity and a choice to make, not just as parents, but as humans. Regardless of intention, we will influence others, so it's up to you as to what kind of impact you want to have. This requires us to look beyond ourselves, to recognize that no matter what your job title, level of education, childhood experiences, etc., we all have something to learn from one another. For this, there is no prerequisite, you can come as you are, imperfect and broken or whole and confident. Remember that change starts from within your own heart, and home, and we carry that out into our communities. I want to encourage others to lead an intentional life and be the role model, because you never know who is watching and learning something from you.

Callie Jo Knapp

RYAN ROGERS

"Be the light!"

If a T-Shirt Could Talk…

About Me

Ryan N. Rogers served with distinction for almost 11 years in the United States Marine Corps, serving on 5 deployments, including one to Iraq and once to Afghanistan. From humble beginnings born and raised in southern Ohio. His father was a businessman and his mother stayed at home raising him and his three other brothers. When we were young, sports and competition were held in high regard. My Dad always impressed upon us the power of competition growing up. Not standing for poor sportsmanship and bullying. Most times he was either the head coach of "said sports team" or at least an assistant coach. This did not afford my brothers and me the ability to slack off and not always give 100 percent. At least not without repercussion.

The catalyst for my service in the USMC was solidified on September 11, 2001. I was a sophomore in high school when they wheeled in a box T.V. and we watched the second tower get hit. We watched as American citizens jumped from extreme heights to their deaths, just to escape the fire and hell that others were succumbing to. The feelings and calling that ensued following that day in history set me on a path to the middle east. From that day forward, there was nothing I wanted more than to become a Marine and serve on the front lines with my brothers. Dealing out American resolve and revenge for the acts in 2001. Enlisting shortly after high school graduation, I was on my way to a whole new life. I went to boot camp in September of "04" and then to SOI. Following the School of Infantry, I checked in to the Basic Security Guard school in Chesapeake, VA. Following this school, I was assigned to the 3rd F.A.S.T. (fleet anti-terrorism security team) Company. I rotated into one of the most senior platoons, due to 2 drug pops. My roommate Eric Chavez and I were the replacements for these poor souls. I checked in just after the platoon conducted a refuel defuel mission for nuclear submarines, and we were working up for a deployment to Guantanamo Bay, Cuba.
Following the GTMO deployment, we rotated into southeast Asia as a quick reaction force QRF for all the embassies in the Area of Responsibility. We would be the first on scene likely if something happened at one of the embassies in the region. Not long into the deployment Hezbollah and

Wisdom of Heroes

Israel got after it with one another. We were activated and conducted a noncombatant operation with members of the Marine Expeditionary Unit that was afloat for similar reasons. We conducted one of the largest NEOs in the modern-day.

Next, I checked into the 3rd Battalion 2nd Marines, Lima Company. I was promoted to Corporal and took command of my first squad. I learned the ropes of leading a squad on our following deployment to Iraq. Not much of a kinetic fight, but great IED and patrolling experience. Following this deployment, I tried out for the All-Marine Boxing team. I made the team and fought for the Marines for almost 10 months. I went 5 and 1, with one no contest.

Following my bid on the boxing team, I re-enlisted for an OPFOR bonus (operational forces) and was assigned to 3rd Battalion 6th Marines, Kilo Company. As a Squad Leader in the Second Platoon, we invaded the Taliban stronghold of Marjah and fought hard for the entirety of the pump. Detailed in the book Lions of Marjah, which was released in April Last year.

After Marjah, I was a combat instructor at the school of infantry where I began to excel professionally and struggle personally. I was retired medically on the last day of 2014 with a severe TBI and bilateral hearing loss, among other things. Since retirement, I have earned an AA with honors as well as a BA in Homeland Security (Magna Cum Laude). I also released my war memoir "Lions of Marjah" and started the Choices Not Chances Podcast. I have recently made multiple trips to Camp Lejeune to conduct PMEs on my book and to deliver Keynote speeches to the active-duty Marines. My entire platform, from the book to the podcast and the speaking events is to better the warfighter. Not only the warfighters currently in uniform. But the ones of past battles, there is much to be learned.

If a T-Shirt Could Talk...

From Ryan Rogers' Interview
(Episode #217)

STACY JOHNSTON: "So with all that you've walked through, from this little boy in North Carolina to this gentleman that you stand as today holding this space for people to just get better in your space and own where they are. Using all the words that there are, Ryan, what is your one line statement to the world? What does your t-shirt say?"

RYAN ROGERS: "Be the light. Be the light. There's enough hate and there's enough darkness in the world; we need the light. I tell my kids that every day."

STACY JOHNSTON: "That's beautiful."

CASSEY HOLLAND: "You can't fight darkness with darkness, only light can do that."

RYAN ROGERS: "Yeah, I think it was John Stewart Mill that said in a university speech, 'The only way for evil to succeed is to the indifference of good men.' Actually, I think what he said is, "bad men need nothing more to accomplish their needs than that good people should look on and do nothing." And in the world in which we live, there's too many times that people are you know, let's just call them downright assholes. You got somebody that's just not nice to somebody and then people see that let's go with bullying, bullying in school. You know, I'd say a good 70% of kids know that bullying is wrong, but they don't want to get involved. People are non confrontational. We have this world that has become technologically advanced to the point where everything is done on screens, and I got out of the Marine Corps after 10 years and went to college. You know, I had to be a better writer. I had to sharpen my mind. I had to get good so I could communicate to people and I go on to the campuses and the newer generations won't even look at you in the face when you walk and I would you know give the proper greeting of the day and say you know, hey, how are you doing? Even though they wouldn't look at me and they would almost look down and scurry away that they were afraid to get engaged in conversation and when that's what we have coming up. Those are the people that are going to be leading. It's scary. We really need to STEMI that and and until people eight when you see something that's wrong, you correct that. When you see somebody being mistreated you correct that. That's what our principles as a country are, that's what we stand for is not oppressing people, not bullying people. And you know, I just think that far too often we have people that are good men and women that look on and then do nothing by way of intervening in the situation. Be the light."

STACY JOHNSTON: "I love that. I believe that the moment you decide to make that decision and own that grand overall design in your place in that, you've got this light to shine. If the only time you ever shine your light is in a room full of other people shining their light, how bright is that light?"
RYAN ROGERS: "What are you changing? You're not brightening any darkness? Another big thing is that so much stuff is too partisan these days. You have the social media platforms and everybody's playing for a vote for their side and everybody forgot to have conversations with each other or even what a conversation was. You know, if you come into to a talk and you already are set in your ways, and you have no intention of learning anything from the other person, that's not really a conversation. You know, we should all go in open minded and hear each other out and try to advance for the greater good. Not just come in with our own beliefs and, you know, respond, you know, wait for somebody to talk, stop talking to respond instead of listening to them."

STACY JOHNSTON: "Amen. Amen. What a beautiful point. I don't know about anybody else but I've got two pages of notes already, 10 bumper stickers. It's great. It's been a great day for me! And I do soundly believe this. Those who need to hear this message will hear it. I just think that's the way it works out and I'm going to continue to believe that."

If a T-Shirt Could Talk...

Dear Reader:

Greetings,

I'm here today to talk to you about the chase. The chase is the journey, let's say. Regardless of your economic standing, we all must travel along and decide what to make of the journey. The choice is yours, as to what you make of that journey. When I was young, I was very competitive in sports, I excelled more on the field than I did in the classroom and had my fair share of poor decisions. I was a sophomore in high school when the attacks on 9/11 occurred, and I watched the falling man live on a television that was wheeled into the classroom. The events of 9/11 cemented my future as a U.S. Marine. I deployed 5 times, my last one in 2010, to Helmand River Valley Province to invade an area called Marjah. On that deployment, we lost Marines, the first I had lost while on the field making decisions. This really rocked my psyche, but in many ways for the better. I began to scribble some notes in my journal on that deployment and when I came home, began to write a book. I was medically retired in 2014, and for the first time in my adult life woke up without a purpose. With a mission, with a complete loss with what my life had become. I needed the mission. I needed the chaos, I needed the chase

    Sure, I was still a young father and a husband, and that purpose is huge, the biggest, but it seemed all of what I attached my personality to was removed from me. I was an infantry Marine with a decade of war in my past. I always had a mission and a purpose that was on a life-or-death scale. I always had something to chase.
I decided that my children need more from me than being "retired." I knew that I needed to be on the chase, and it didn't matter what mission at the time.

    See when you live your life in service to others, your external motivators are what get you by when things get tough, or when you become lost. My family needed me to be more. I started college and started doing homework at the table with my kids. I went back to school with the sole purpose of becoming a better writer and a better speaker. As I continued with my AA, I got back to writing my book as well. The biggest thing I learned at the community college, was how little I knew about the world around me.

Next was the BA. Why would I stop? I have kids to feed, a wife to support, and a life to support. There is no time to slow down, there is no time to lay up in the house, and there is no time to pass on opportunities. My external motivators were ever-present and growing fast. Not to mention the chase felt so good while I was getting my associates. I needed more. I graduated and began a BA program in Homeland Security. I knew I wanted to stay in the vein of my former profession and stay current and up to date with the ways of National security. I graduated in 18 months with my degree Magna Cum Laude. One of the external motivators for school was my mother. I promised my mother the day I left for boot camp in 2004 that I would get my degree with the benefits earned. So back to the chase. Was it easy? No! But it was an investment in my future. There is no price too high for the future of my family. And the chase again, though harder than ever, felt right. When I'm chasing my success the anxiety of the world falls away.

Now that I had school behind me, I transitioned back to my book. It was published a few months following my graduation date. I had doubled down on it for a few months and invested in the project. When publishers didn't chomp at the bit to represent my book, it meant nothing to me. The chase had reinvigorated my spirit, and I was chasing that success harder now than ever, with opportunities arising. I Didn't care that they didn't believe in the work and the process, I had mouths to feed and people to inspire. I had my external motivators staring at me, watching me, needing me to grind.

They said that the average self-published author sells about 15-350 copies lifetime… I sold that in the first week! I didn't need anyone else to motivate me, I need them to believe in me. When they didn't, I said roger that. No factor. I'm chasing though! I going to chase my success.
Do you want to know where success is found?

If a T-Shirt Could Talk...

It Is found in the chase…You must grind and if you don't commit to the chase and leave your foot on the accelerator, you don't stand a chance. You must grind out success and leave the demons that plague you behind. I told my wife a while back, I said, the safest I ever feel is when I am in motion. Be it in a car, a plane, a boat, running on my feet, or working out. The grind is my safe space. And you know what that is, don't you? That is my unconscious mind, being at ease on the chase. So long as I am on the chase, the demons stay behind me. My shortcomings, my failures, my addictions…. You know what they say about addiction right? They say addiction is the killer of ambition. Stay on the chase, stay grinding, and never get comfortable, make discomfort your comfort zone, success is found in the work you put into the chase.

—Ryan Rogers

DEVIN TOMIAK

"Be emphatic"

If a T-Shirt Could Talk...

About Me/Contact Me

Devin Tomiak, Founder
thebiggiescards.com

From Dwan Devin Tomiak's Interview
(Episode #220)

STACY JOHNSON: "If there was a one liner that you could put on a tshirt as your message to the world, what would it say?"

DEVIN TOMIAK: "I think it would say, 'Be empathetic.' I used to think that empathy was this hyped up version of sympathy, right? It's just this ability to put yourself in another person's shoes, but to be empathetic means to be able to notice the subtle verbal and nonverbal signals that people give off, that let you know what they need or want. Empathy is important because it is what enables us to connect with others."

Closing Statement: "I think reliance is about connection, but ultimately it's about love. Connection and love are at the heart of the matter really, resilient people keep going and it's because they love. They love themselves or something that keeps them headed forward. Maybe it's something like bird watching, ping pong, being in service to others. Maybe they love another person deeply. But at the end of the day it's love or connection, or whatever you want to call it, and then you have resilience."

If a T-Shirt Could Talk...

Dear Reader:

I was so honored to be a guest on Un-Caped Heroes and now I feel even more proud to be a part of Stacy and Cassey's book. With each of their conversations, they sow connection, something I feel especially passionate about myself. It has been such a gift to have crossed paths with them and such a joy to have been able to tell my story to their community. Life can be hard and complicated. Often the most we can do is to learn from each other. Sharing my discoveries and learning have brought meaning to my days, and if I've touched a single person in a positive way, I am grateful. Seven years ago, losing a brother to suicide as a young mother set me on a journey to build resilience in my children. But I found that teaching my kids resilience was not exactly a straightforward endeavor. It felt daunting and confusing. When I searched for a tool to help me, I came up empty-handed. So I enlisted the help of a 20-year veteran of community psychology and together we created The Biggies Conversation Cards, a research-based card deck for parents, teachers and caregivers that make it fun and easy to meaningfully connect with elementary-aged children, while growing their emotional intelligence and confidence, fostering their communication skills, and building their resilience.

BOYD HAMLIN

"Act like you. You're the only one that can."

If a T-Shirt Could Talk...

About Me

Boyd Hamlin has spent 20+ years developing successful youth ministries and 12 years in church planting. He has encountered 2 brain surgeries and lives with Transverse Myelitis. Boyd understands Service, Struggle and Surrender and the lessons it teaches us to become better versions of ourselves. He is a trainer, coach and an award-winning speaker. Boyd has also developed The Hero Builder system that helps people uncover the Hero inside of them, theherobuilder.com. He is dedicated to helping young and old alike strengthen their ACTiTUDE. He and his wife, Melanie, live in the Phoenix area and have two grown boys.

Boyd Hamlin, The HERO Builder
Founder | The Hero Builder program
Email: boyd@theherobuilder.com
Cellphone: 505-850-5600
Website: theherobuilder.com

Wisdom of Heroes

From Boyd Hamlin's Interview
(Episode #222)

CASSEY HOLLAND: "Boyd, if there was a one liner that you could put on a t-shirt as your message to the world, what would it say?"

BOYD HAMLIN: "I think the thing that I would say because this is what I'm hearing out there right now too is I would say, 'Act Like You. You're the only one who can.' The world needs the true you."

STACY JOHNSTON: "I like it. I like that."

BOYD HAMLIN: "They don't need to be everybody else. We already have one of those. They need to be themselves. The world needs you to be you. One of the things that is so significant is how in the world do I become the true me? You're around at least five people in what I call the circle of five in your life that brings out the greatness in you. That doesn't tell you that your greatness comes by being somebody else. They bring out the greatness in you and that's who I'm looking for in my life is five people to help me bring out the true me so I can be that Boyd better."

CASSEY HOLLAND: "I heard a gentleman say the other day that you'll never be number one trying to be somebody else. You'll always just be a second rate number two."

BOYD HAMLIN: "Oh, wow."

CASSEY HOLLAND: "I was like , 'Ooh! Ouch!'"

BOYD HAMLIN: "Who wants to deal with that crap? I don't! You know the other thing too, ladies, at the end when this is all over we are not accountable to God by being somebody else. We're not Oh, I was the best Joe that I could be. I was the best Bobby that I could be. You're going to be accountable to being the best you that He made you to be. And it's just that simple."

If a T-Shirt Could Talk...

STACY JOHNSTON: "Yep, it is that simple. It's so hard. It's so simple it's difficult, right? And I think we make it difficult when it really could be just so simple."

BOYD HAMLIN: "I was asked by a kid the other day, she said, "How do I be me?" You kept saying that there is a hero in me for the world to see, so how do I be me? I said Oh, that's easy. I said, if the Incredible Hulk woke up one morning and he looked in the mirror and he said, 'well, I just don't want to be the Hulk today. I'd rather be Wonder Woman.' Does that make any sense? She says, 'no.' I said well, what if Wonder Woman woke up that very same morning and she said, 'you know what? I don't want to be Wonder Woman today. I want to be Superman.' Does that make any sense? She said no, it doesn't. I said, what makes sense? She said, I've got to be the Hulk if I'm the Hulk. I said exactly. And you are the only person who can be you. So be the best you that you can be and having the right people around us is going to help us to do that."

STACY JOHNSTON: "That's a great story. That's great!"

Wisdom of Heroes

Dear Reader:

When you are the hero in your own story, you're in the wrong story. When it comes to heroes, there are the kind that inspire us to be all that we can be. This kind of hero is usually difficult to access other than the books they write and the certification programs they provide. Then, there's the other kind of hero that walks with you on your journey, helping you become the best that you can be, giving you their time, talents, undivided attention and all the additional help you can handle, if you're open to it. They provide you with wisdom from the road they've traveled, encouragement to keep walking on your journey, get excited for you when things are looking up and are there to hand you a tissue or extend a hug when things take a downward turn. You never have to knock on their door because the door is always open. A pot of coffee is put on to talk through your current journey and give you hope to keep walking the road of your journey that lies ahead. Most likely, they will be on the road with you. These are the kind of people, heroes, are world is lacking and needing more of. These are the kind of heroes we should strive to be more like. The kind that helps others see their own story and are willing to help in the process. These are the un-caped heroes that know that if they live their story well, you will talk about them in yours. Their payment is simple – your success! Even though you may not feel like a hero without a cape, just be reminded that the success that you have helped others attain, however big or small, IS your cape! Strive to always be the un-caped hero in others stories.

If a T-Shirt Could Talk...

RICHARD POWELL

"If you're not planning your life, someone else will."

If a T-Shirt Could Talk...

About Me

Earth Wind Fire Water Training and Development The Headdress stands for the 11 Leadership Skills:
Communication, Resources, Needs, Representing, Example, Planning, Performance, Evaluating, Effective Instruction, Delegation, Personal Growth.

The Square is the 4 Directions:
Earth = Grounded, Wind = Change, Fire = Passion, Water = Reinvention

The Gator is our Clan with an arrow pointing upwards. Asking, What's Next?

Website: www.EWFW.org

Wisdom of Heroes

From Richard Powell's Interview
(Episode #223)

STACY JOHNSTON: "Okay, so let's turn the wheel a little bit and let's take this a little different path. We've learned some things about you and the wisdom that you have to share and the knowledge that you share around. So let's put you back on the pedestal for a minute. And let's put the cape back on you and help you recognize that you are probably more people's hero in a day than you recognize. And so thank you for the space you provide, the wisdom you provide, and just that place people can come and learn and get better in your presence."

RICHARD POWELL: "Thank you."

STACY JOHNSTON: "You're very welcome. So, with that cape soundly snapped on, flying, this is your opportunity, taking the world as your stage "of all the things that are and all the words their are, what is your one liner to the world? What does your t-shirt say?"

RICHARD POWELL: "Gosh, I actually wrote it down but I really think it's that, 'If you're not planning your life someone else is and will.' Or it could be to build your own library. Read, listen and ask questions and then share it with others. That's been my motto. Research is fine, but you've got to take action and do something. You've got to take action on it. And that's the hard part because some people won't be ready when you're ready to take care of them. Some people have to go and think about it and come back and say I'm ready now. I've done a lot of life coaching and those kinds of things in my career, and some people when they're not ready, you cannot fill them up. It just doesn't work. They have to be ready to be filled. You can't be Mr. Miyagi when you don't have a Daniel."

STACY JOHNSTON: "There you go! Absolutely, absolutely. Richard, it's been such a beautiful experience having you here with us today. And thank you so much for just taking the time out of your day, for your honesty, for your knowledge and wisdom being willing to share it."

If a T-Shirt Could Talk...

Dear Reader:

First Steps

Vision (Your Future Picture)
Take time to sit with a pad and pen. Write down, draw what your life will look like. What are you feeling? What do you smell? Where are you living? What vehicle you own? Who is with you?

Mission (Your Passion / Calling)
Discover your passion, you're calling. Search for a mentor to help you do this. It is not always an easy thing, and you very well might have to do it through trial and error.

Strategy (Your Plan)
Your plan is a daily, weekly, monthly, and yearly written set of what needs done and when it needs completed. Use a year calendar with the most important dates written in. Then use your daily, weekly, and monthly check lists to ensure each one is completed on time or before they are due.

The 11 Leadership Skills
1.   Communication:
Too much is better than too little. Share what you learn, what you know, and everyone wins. Communicating is more than just words. Over 70% of communication is non-verbal. So, a question might be: What is the message you are sending even before you start to speak?

2. Resources:
Know who can do what, when, where, and how will make you the "go to person." These resources could be the person, the tool, the company, the resources, that you need to move ahead. Who do you know and what can they bring to the table?

3. Characteristics and Needs of the Group and Its Members:
Know what the other person(s) are made up of. There are many tools and questions to discover the passions, the dreams, the capabilities, the attitudes, of those around you.

Know who you can count on for different things.

4. Represent the Team:
You will be called upon to represent the team either in a formal situation or at the water cooler. Know what can be shared and what should not be shared. Know how to explain things in the simplest terms and forms. Einstein said, "If you cannot explain it simply, you do not know it well enough." Be a positive face for the group.

5. Set the Example:
People do what people see. Not what they hear, but what they see. If you say one thing and act another way, your credibility is lost, and it will be a long road to rebuild it. People follow the direction you go, not the one you point. Someone is always looking.

6. Planning:
Planning is a daily activity! When we fail to plan – we plan to fail. Everyone and every organization needs a Vision. When they have that in place the plan is a road map of how to get there. The plan allows for taking some different roadways and still follow the vision that will get you to your destination.

7. Team Performance:
Every team must have metrics in place. If not, then how will you know when you get there and how will you know how to do it again. Metrics allow you to better evaluate if the plan is a good one or maybe that alternate route would be better.

8. Evaluate:
Grandpa said, "Evaluate everything!" What he meant was to stop and think it through. What is going well? What did not go so well? What needs to be added? What needs to be left behind? Grandpa also said, "If done daily, you will always be moving ahead!"

9. Effective Instruction:
"Each one - instruct one" is by far the best method. I do, you watch. I do, you help. You do, I help. You do, I watch. You show someone else. Remember that "People do what people see!"

10. Delegation:
The mark of a great leader is delegation. When we do everything ourselves, it sends the message to the team they are not trusted, and they are not capable or worthy of being involved.

11. Personal Growth:
Ongoing continuous personal growth will require a plan for yourself. Set on your calendar dates for reflection, rejuvenation, books to be read, seminars to be a part of, and encourage those around you to have a plan of action also.

ALEX PIN

"If there are no roads, go make one!"

If a T-Shirt Could Talk...

About Me/Contact Me

Email: alex@alexpin.info
Phone: +386 (0)69 729 403
Website: alexpin.info

Wisdom of Heroes

From Alex Pin's Interview
(Episode #229)

STACY JOHNSON: "If you had a one liner to the world, to put on your tshirt, as your message to the world, what would it say and why?"

ALEX PIN: "'If there are no roads, go and make one.' Go and create your own one, because everyone has their own path. Yeah, you can see someone's road and they're moving, and you can learn on someone's road. But in life, everyone needs to make their own one, and you just go and create it. It doesn't matter if you don't see it, you just go and do it. There has always been someone in life, someone in history looking back, if there are no roads, someone came to pave the road. So just go and build, and create your own one. If there are no roads, go and create your own one."

Closing Statement: "Thank you for having me, that's the first thing. When it comes to a moment you just don't know where to step, what to do, if there is a solution or not…just close your eyes, breathe in, exhale, open your eyes, and it's in your moment. The solution will come."

If a T-Shirt Could Talk...

Dear Reader:

Being a bold WOW Mom

Each and every one of us carries a legacy of experience, pain, beliefs and patterns. When raising children, we always raise ourselves first. When we get caught in a circle of these thoughts, patterns or "badgers" as I like to call them, we lose the connection to ourselves. We lose our calmness and awareness, and we lose our presence in the given moment.
It's always good to know yourself and your wishes. Therefore is important that you answer this question and really write it down:

WHAT KIND OF A MOM YOU WANNA BE?
You being you. And you have to have some boldness in you to go out here and be who you are not someone else. That's making your own path.

Sometimes we feel so powerless that we scream and get angry in order to make kids listen to us. But we also scream on ourselves inside. That scream is the loudest of all.
Its you calling your soul. Its you calling you life Its you calling and awakening your inner power to stand up and be bold and WOW MOM.

Be you. Be bold. We WOW. Be alive.
Alex Pin (www.mywowlife.eu)

TOBEY GEISE

"You have all the answers within."

If a T-Shirt Could Talk...

About Me

https://www.tghealingworks.com/

Tobey Geise is a lifelong student, always seeking and evolving. She began her personal growth path in 2004, diving deep into self-awareness and transformational work. Her growth path led her to spirituality, where she overcame a painful eating disorder and turned her attention to healing her mind, body, and soul.

A certified Integrative NLP Coach, Master Practitioner of Hypnotherapy and Mental and Emotional Release®, Reiki Master, and Breathwork Practitioner, Tobey is passionate about empowering others to find their own healing within.

Thank you!

Big Love and Gratitude!

Tobey Geise
Soul Expansion Coach

e: tobey@tghealingworks.com
w: www.tghealingworks.com

Wisdom of Heroes

From Tobey Geise's Interview
(Episode #247)

STACY JOHNSON: "So if you were going to give a one liner of advice that you would put on a tshirt for the world to read, what would it say?"

TOBEY: "You have all the answers to honor everyone where they're at on their journey. we can judge somebody else, or get mad at somebody for doing something that we don't like, but we have no idea what that person is going through, what that person has experienced in their life, in their day, and why they're acting in a way that displeases us. But we are not the only ones. Look into another humans eyes—see them, really see them. honoring God and everyone else. That's what namaste means the God in me the God in you. We are all the same. We are all on the same path. We are all in the human experience. Some people have different knowledge or are more experienced than others in different areas, but we are all in this together. Just honoring everyone for the journey that they're on. I guess my tshirt would say, your journey."

If a T-Shirt Could Talk...

Dear Reader:

We are much much more than our physical bodies. We have been guided in our society and culture to focus so much on the outside package, our appearances, whether that's our physical bodies or the clothes that we're wearing, what we drive, etc., but that's not what life is about. Life is what is on the inside, and there is so much magic within each and every one of us. So much magic. I can't even begin to explain to you how amazing this human experience is, how everyone has the opportunity to see and experience life in this way.

OLIVIA COOK

"Go be a bad-ass!"

If a T-Shirt Could Talk...

About Me

Olivia Cook is a certified Transformational Success Coach & NLP Practitioner, podcast host and motivational speaker. She helps service-based female entrepreneurs and content creators build habits to reach their next level of success. Focusing on productivity, mindset and using their menstrual cycles to their benefits. Her clients are able to increase their income, reduce their stress levels and enjoy their success journey.

Her podcast, The Empowered Woman Badass & Unfiltered was made to inspire, empower and educate. It showcases badass women from all over the world. Providing tips on business, personal development, mindset and healing.

She is the co-founder of the Christ-driven brand, Relentless Glory. A brand whose purpose is to spread the word of God through motivation, education and praise.

Olivia is also a Christian, military wife and humanitarian. She actively gives back to her community.

From Olivia Cook"s Interview
(Episode #272)

STACY JOHNSON: "If you had a one liner, to put out to the world as your statement of advice, what would your tshirt say, and why?"

OLIVIA COOK: "The first thing that came to my mind is, 'Go out and be a badass!' That's my tagline for my podcast. But that's what I really like to tell people, you know, just to go out and be the best version of themselves."

Closing Statement: "I just want to let each of you know that is listening, that you have a light. And it is so important to shine it. There are so many people that just do the same thing all the time, and do what other people say, but they don't make an impact in this world. If you're listening to this, you have an impact to make. So like I said before, go out and be a badass."

If a T-Shirt Could Talk...

Dear Reader:

When I was coming up for the title for my podcast, I wanted to find a word the perfectly described the women that were my guests. I wanted something bold, a little edgy and memorable. I knew my guests weren't going to be average. The name helped me attract the women I was looking for. They were trailblazers. From running businesses, serving their communities, adding value to the lives they impact, to taking care of themselves and their loved ones. Sharing their truth open and honestly.

It's been 1.5 years since launching and my guests have not only empowered my listeners but myself as well. From leaving an abusive relationship and now helping other women leave their abuser's, to helping end homelessness, to helping over 140 flee from Ukraine. Just to name some of the things my guests have done. These women are making history and saving lives.

The American philosopher Ralph Emerson said, "To be yourself in a world that is constantly trying to make you something else is an accomplishment." To me being a badass is about making a positive impact in the world while unapologetically being yourself. It takes guts and grit to go against societal norms and be yourself.

Now more than ever it's time for everyone to be empowered to contribute to the betterment of our society. Everyone is gifted in their own unique way. They just have to believe it for themselves. So not only in my podcast but in my business and everyday life I aim to empower others to become the best version of themselves. With that being said, "Go out and be a Badass!"

CASSEY HOLLAND

"Give yourself grace."

If a T-Shirt Could Talk...

About Me

Hello from West Texas. I am Cassey Holland and I am the face behind Guided By Grace. I wear many hats. I am a Christian, a Wife and a mom. I am an Internationally certified speaker coach and trainer. I run a small business out of my home in West Texas and I homeschool 3 small kids. I think if I had one small bit of advice for everyone reading this book it would be… Give yourself some Grace.

Wisdom of Heroes

From Cassey Holland's Interview
(Episode #294)

STACY JOHNSON: "Let's turn the tables on you Cassey, let's pretend like you're the her ofor today, and you're on your pedestal. Number one, I would like for you to take amoment to realize that you are probably more people's hero than you realize. I hope that you recognize that. Thank you for what you do, for the services you provide. Onyour pedestal with your cape firmly in place, what is your onliner, what does your tshirt say?"

CASSEY HOLLAND: "'Give yourself grace.' We're the hardest, we are our own worst enemy. We are the hardest on ourselves. We see problems with ourselves that I guarantee you 99.98% aren't even noticed. We block our own blessing faster than anybody because we are so hard on ourselves. Sometimes you just have to give yourself a little grace and realize that it is okay."

Donna Marie Closing Statement: "I would say heroes are human and they inspire through a human connection, and a hero is a person that emerges on the other side of a struggle. They pave the way for those that wish to follow and I am grateful to have met Cassey today. She is a hero."

If a T-Shirt Could Talk...

Dear Reader:

Grace is the one thing that is so easy for us to give everyone else but seems impossible to give ourselves sometimes. We have to remember that we are all human and its ok to not be ok. Its ok to normalize plan B. Its ok. Society would have us believe that our value increases based on our accomplishments, but the truth is…our value has always been priceless, no matter our accomplishments.

Repeat After Me.
I am Amazing.
I am Strong.
I am Brave.
I am Enough.
Stay Guided By Grace.

Cass

PAUL KENNEDY

"Travel. Now!"

If a T-Shirt Could Talk...

About Me

For the past thirty years Paul has been working in the restaurant business, bringing together delicious foods and atmospheres where customers could create their own memories. Growing up in Northern Virginia, Paul went off to study hospitality management at East Carolina University, followed by culinary arts at Johnson & Wales University. After his education he departed to New York City where he continued to establish himself in the restaurant world, while also homing in on his love of writing and photography.

In 2018, with a backpack and some inspiration, Paul cashed in his proverbial chips and took off to see the world. The inspiration clearly worked because he never returned. His journey of uncertainty found it's purpose of exploring what the world has to offer. Paul has written a cookbook about the food and culture of Vietnam. Besides authentic Vietnamese recipes, Paul hopes to do his part in piquing the readers' interest in understanding the world, in any aspect. Once you do that, he feels like everyone will understand each other.

Wisdom of Heroes

From Paul Kennedy's Interview
(Episode #300)

STACY JOHNSON: "If you had one line of advice to give to the world, what would it be? What would your t-shirt say?"

PAUL KENNEDY: "Probably Travel. Now. Travel Now. Travel Now. That is the key to everything that we are talking about. That's the key. That's the key to everything. It's how I achieved empathy, how I learned all this. I wouldn't have learned if I didn't make that step, if I didn't travel solo. I didn't vacation, I traveled. I traveled; big difference. I'm not saying travel to 7-eleven and get a big gulp. I'm not saying travel to the local beach. I am saying go somewhere by yourself. You know the cost of the flight from Charleston to New York used to cost more than the flight from New York to Hanoi. So yes, financially if you can afford that flight to New York to Charleston, then you can afford to travel to a country like Viet Nam. A hotel in Viet Nam you could stay for a month, for the same price as one night in New York City. But I know not everyone has the ability to travel, but you can still travel somewhere locally by yourself. It's almost like a meditation. If you travel somewhere by yourself, not using your Marriott points but you actually go somewhere and get lost, not lost in the mountains where you're dehydrated for thirty days, but somewhere you can wander and kind of learn from a different culture. So if you live in the south, then up north. Obviously the more different the culture is the more you'll learn. T-shirt, Travel Now. Unlock all of this. Unlock your passion."

Closing Statement: "I agree with Cassey, step out of your comfort zone, make change, find your passion. And send me your photo on twitter, send it to me! In all honesty, if anyone ever wants inspiration or has questions about travel, I would always be willing to answer any questions that I know. I didn't know anyone that traveled, I didn't have a passport, I was lucky to have friends that did this. I am more than willing to help anyone out with any advice that I can give. Reach out to me."

If a T-Shirt Could Talk...

Dear Reader:

To appreciate the culture, you must understand the food. To appreciate the food, you must understand the culture.
- Paul B. Kennedy

SNAPSHOT

For $35 you can buy a one-way airline ticket across the country. Teachers are underpaid here, too; most make $250 US dollars a month, around minimum wage in Viet Nam. Street venders make $130 US a month, so don't offer them less money than they ask. Quitting before Tet is a common problem because employees want time off around the holiday. Being a police officer carries prestige and often requires nepotism or an exchange of money. Police 'fine' drunk drivers by making them do pushups on the side of the road. Here, people don't stay home for 'snow days', but they do for heavy 'rain days.' In US dollars, it costs $4 to have a tech come to your house to replace the toner on your printer. Teeth cleaning and x-rays cost $8 total for both, or you can get a $3 haircut and shave. Want a pet? Miniature Pinschers go for $22. Ball point pens cost .13 cents apiece. A car wash is $2.20, but a motorbike wash is only .88 cents. For $2.40 you could buy a loaf of bread and a dozen duck eggs, but lobster, at this moment, costs $45 a pound. All you can eat at a restaurant will run you between $6.62 and $15.45 per person and fresh coconut water is $1.33/quart. A religion, or shall we call it a cult called the Coconut Religion was founded in Vietnam,. It's practice called for only consuming coconuts and drinking only coconut milk. Author John Steinbeck's son, John Steinbeck IV, was a follower.

STACY JOHNSTON

*"Write the story. Dance the dance.
Take the bow."*

About Me

Stacy Johnston owns and operates Enlighten Up, a personal consulting firm based in Texas. Stacy is an internationally certified personal development coach, consultant, speaker, and trainer. Stacy spends her time guiding individuals, families, companies and communities to recognize the power of their influence and the importance of the legacy they leave behind. Her focus is personal character and integrity and building your business or family from the inside out. She is also a contributing author to the Amazon #1 best seller, Caged No More. Stacy grew up in a dance studio family and was blessed to enjoy the beautiful world of the arts all of her life. Stacy is over 30 years married to a wonderful man with whom she has three children and a growing number of grandchildren. Stacy owned and operated Applause School of Dance for thirty years, took a pivot, and spent eleven years in the adolescent/adult substance abuse and mental health profession as a family services specialist. Outside of her business practice, her new joy is co-hosting two podcasts, Un-Caped Heroes and Mid-Week Mind Candy.

You can connect with Stacy at:
Facebook.com/StacyO.Johnston or Enlightenup.stacyj@gmail.com
For podcast information reach out to: Herobuilder2020@gmail.com

Wisdom of Heroes

From Stacy Johnston's Interview
(Episode #311)

CASSEY: "So, if you could put a one liner of advice as your statement to the world on a t-shirt, what would it say? And why?"

STACY JOHNSTON: "My t-shirt would say 'Write the Story, Dance the Dance, Take the Bow.' My belief, life according to Stacy 101, I believe with all the stars, and all the animals and all the food in the world, God still decided the world needed one of you. And there's a reason for that. If you never take the opportunity to recognize that you get to write the story, you've been gifted this life and this opportunity, what's that about for you? Write the story. We spend so much time letting everybody else write our story for us, with undisclosed permission, we just woke up one day and we're doing it. Just get up in the morning, drink the cup of coffee and dance the dance that someone else has programmed for us to do that day. And we forget that it's our dance, it's our story, write the story. You have to believe that your story is valuable; if you weren't valuable, you wouldn't be here. You're valuable, your story could be somebody else's survival guide. It matters. We're ingrained to believe that self growth and becoming the best you possible and finding out is selfish. How dare you take that time away from your family, or your business, or your life, or your job. We're happy with you just the way you are, so we go 'okay.' And we don't. We never get to see you dance, you've given up your best dance for someone else to perform. Why? Write the story, write the song, dance your dance, take the bow, it's yours. So my t-shirt would say 'Write the story. Dance the dance. Take the bow.'"

Closing Statement: "Thank you both, it's odd to be on the other side of this microphone and share, I can't think of anyone I'd be more comfortable with to do this with, so thank-you for this opportunity, this time to share. I just want the listening audience and the world to recognize where there's up, there's down, where there is in, there is out. For as much darkness, despair, strife or stress, you'll see an equal measure of beautiful on the other side. Find the daylight, find the shine, find the place that resonates with your heart. It's such an honor to be here, and I get to share time with them today.

If a T-Shirt Could Talk…

So just remember it's your story. Write the story, sing the song, dance the dance, and then take the final bow."

Dear Reader:

Underneath the Music

Life has a rhythm. A song to sing and a dance to perform. We are life. One day, the Grand Overall Designer looked around and decided the world needed one of You. At that moment, you were gifted with a story to write, a song to sing, and a dance to dance. This story is your legacy, its words and wisdom becoming the lyrics to your song. And then you dance. Choices, circumstances, honor and fear, laughter, courage, joy and pain are all instruments in the orchestra of your life. You choose along the way to merely dance to the music, left to its own devices, the consequences deciding your beat. Or, by grace and acceptance, with courage and integrity, you can choose to be the conductor of your own symphony and the choreographer of your dance. After all, it's your song. It's your dance. Sing the song. Dance the dance. Take the final bow.

All too often, culture and environment teach us to exist within the norm, "Please, in the box you go," and we comply. It starts slowly and without much notice. Not by any direct fault or weakness, we allow our family, spouse or partner, children, career and economic status, and even our social media standing, to write our story for us. In time, and with our unspoken permission, they begin to orchestrate our song and control our beat. We get up in the morning, dress in the costume placed neatly on the bed, and dance the dance they have chosen. Time passes, and we hardly notice that we are giving up our best steps up to someone else to perform.

Although we cannot go back and make a new beginning, we can write a different ending. We are often led to believe that our past choices and mistakes have already written our story for us. This is the only song we get to sing. You are dancing your dance. Oh no! I beg to differ. Your journey does not define you; it merely designs you. It is YOUR choice. Underneath the music lies Your rhythm, the tempo of your integrity and the solid cadence of your faith. Show up strong, write the story, sing the song, dance the dance. Then, bow.

Next Steps

Lessons on a Tee is an option you have to turn this book into a unique training opportunity for you personally, your team or organization. This "class" will be customized for your specific need or that of your company or organization. All materials will be pre-approved by the organizing entity.

How it Works:
1) Choose a T- shirt quote from one of the chapters in the book and we will create a training around the chosen statement.
2) 1 quote = 1 hr training
3 quotes = 1/2 day workshop or 3 sessions 6 quotes = A full day or 6 sessions

** Live or virtual options available**
T-Shirts for the quotes chosen will be available through Guided By Grace.
• Stacy Johnston, Cassey Holland and Boyd Hamlin are all Internationally Certified Speakers, coaches and trainers. They work as a team to provide trainings, presentations and team coaching. They each also maintain independent businesses: Enlighten Up, Guided By Grace and The Hero Builder respectively. There are no blanket price sheets. Each training is created specifically to meet the need at hand such as; content, price point, projected outcome, time allowed, mode of delivery, ect.. For questions and/or information, you can contact:
• Stacy Johnston @ Enlightenup.stacyj@gmail.com
• Cassey Holland @ Guidedbygrace21@gmail.com
• Boyd Hamlin @ Boydahamlin@gmail.com

Wisdom of Heroes

Boyd Hamlin

Business: THE HERO BUILDER

The HERO Builder was born with one purpose – to instill hero characteristics and qualities in every child, family, organization, and school that wants to profoundly transform themselves and the world. The HERO Builder journey is a simple one that clearly shines the light on character and how character can be implemented into every aspect of life to improve the individual and those around them.

The Hero Builder can provide a single speaking engagement,
Create a Hero Culture – At Work, Church, School and with your Family
Speaker – Keynotes, Assemblies, Churches, and Youth Groups
Trainer – Building a Hero culture, Character Growth
Coach – one-on-one and group coaching for personal leadership and growth. Creative Consultant
Story/Speech Developer – Discover, Develop and Deliver your story or speech.

For more information on The Hero Builder, visit theherobuilder.com or contact Boyd Hamlin at boyd@theherobuilder.com to start building heroes.

Boyd Hamlin, The HERO Builder
Founder | The Hero Builder program boyd@theherobuilder.com www.theherobuilder.com

If a T-Shirt Could Talk...

Cassey Holland

Guided by Grace is a Personal Consulting Firm based in West Texas, specializing in recovery coaching and mentorship. I myself have been in recovery for 16 years and have developed a very unique perspective on the subject. I provide personal one on one courses and group courses as well. My goal is to assist you in discovering that you have the answers you need already.

My rates are not fixed as everyone has different goals and wants. I can be reached @ GuidedbyGrace21@gmail.com
Be Kind to Yourself.
Stay Guided By Grace.

Stacy Johnston

Stacy Johnston owns and operates Enlighten Up, a personal consulting firm based in Texas. Stacy is an internationally certified personal development coach, consultant, speaker, and trainer. Stacy spends her time guiding individuals, families, companies and communities to recognize the power of their influence and the importance of the legacy they leave behind. Her focus is personal character and integrity and building your business or family from the inside out. She is also a contributing author to the Amazon #1 best seller, Caged No More. Stacy grew up in a dance studio family and was blessed to enjoy the beautiful world of the arts all of her life. Stacy is over 30 years married to a wonderful man with whom she has three children and a growing number of grandchildren. Stacy owned and operated Applause School of Dance for thirty years, took a pivot, and spent eleven years in the adolescent/adult substance abuse and mental health profession as a family services specialist. Outside of her business practice, her new joy is co-hosting two podcasts, Un-Caped Heroes and Mid-Week Mind Candy.

You can connect with Stacy at:
Facebook.com/StacyO.Johnston or Enlightenup.stacyj@gmail.com
For podcast information reach out to: Herobuilder2020@gmail.com

Enlighten Up is business and personal consulting firm serving individuals, groups, businesses, and communities to develop and grow Integrity and Influence.

Services include but are not limited to:

    Master Mind groups
    Personal coaching
    Business coaching / training
    Group coaching/training
    Workshops

If a T-Shirt Could Talk...

Keynotes

There are no brochures or price sheets because each encounter is individualized to your needs and projected outcome.

For more information or to connect to Stacy, send me email to: Enlightenup.stacyj@gmail.com

A special opportunity

One thing we have all learned in this journey that we are on is that it is NEVER just about you. The choices we make and actions we take can and do directly effect other people. With this in mind, we are proud to share a portion of the proceeds from the sale of this book with two fabulous organizations.

GUARDIANS OF THE CHILDREN

AND

THE RIO BRAVO PROJECT

GUARDIANS MISSION STATEMENT

The mission of Guardians of the Children is to recognize and react to child abuse and educate the public to do the same; to serve as advocates to provide strength and stability to families in crisis; and be an answer to the prayer of an abused child or teen for courage, support, and protection.

We serve as a public benefit organization. Our vision is to improve the quality of life in our community by educating the public and making them aware of the steps to take in order to prevent, recognize and react responsibly to the reality of child abuse.

GOC is a Biker Organization also dedicated to protecting the victims of child abuse. Our alliances as Bikers allow us the ability to call upon resources that might not generally be available to the public at large.

We partner with Children Advocacy Agencies, Victim Assistance Groups and others to raise awareness of the prevalence of child abuse. GOC assist these agencies by being one of many resources available to them and introduce the child into our organization where it has been determined it would be beneficial in order to lend support to their family and at the same time protect that child

Our members share a common goal in that we enjoy the open road on our iron horses and are here to convey an important message; 'We stand as one prepared to protect this priceless resource'

"Valor, Truth & Integrity is the Guardian way"

Guardians of the Children was started in 2006 by Ruben "Bamm-Bamm" Cano and Lester "LT" Trevino in San Antonio, Texas and has grown to have Chapters all over the US and Canada.
Website: www.guardiansofthechildren.com

(Q).What is the GOC about?
(A). GOC serves as a public benefit organization. We exist to educate the public about child abuse, and create a safer environment for abused and neglected children including mentoring, helping and supporting children that have been abused, neglected, etc. who have been referred to the GOC by Various agencies or their families.

(Q).Who can join the organization?
(A).Anyone, who shares the same passions to make a difference in a child's life, with the exception of passing a background check first.

(Q).What experience does one need to be a member?
(A).None, only the desire to commit to our cause.

(Q). Do you have to own a motorcycle to join?
(A).You do not have to own one, but you do need to have access to one.

(Q).What if you want to be a part of the organization but not really a member?
(A).We do use the help of non-members on case by case bases for selective events but this is always approved by the president first.

(Q).Will I be able to join in all the events, even if I am a support member?
(A).Yes, as long as you have successfully passed a background check first.

(Q). How long does a new member have to wait in order to get patched?
(A). All members are required to go through a 1 year probationary period prior to being eligible for a patch.

(Q).Are all events mandatory?
(A).Only events declared by the President as such are mandatory.

(Q).Who do I need to speak to about joining?
(A).Each chapters contact information is posted on this website. For membership information contact the Sgt.@Arms of the chapter or the membership coordinator.

(Q).Does this organization get together just to hang out and go for rides?
(A).This organization is here solely for mentoring, helping and supporting children that have been abused, neglected, etc. who have been referred to the GOC by Various agencies or their families. Occasionally we may get together for a fun ride.

(Q).Who would I need to speak to about giving a donation?
(A). Donations should be forwarded to the treasurer of the chapter in your area. There is also a PayPal button for donations on our Homepage.

(Q).Is GOC a 501 © (3) organization?
(A).Yes, we are a Charitable Organization with a 501© (3) status.

(Q).Where does the money go to that is donated and raised for this organization?
(A).All money is used to benefit the mentoring, helping and supporting children that have been abused, neglected, etc. and have been referred to the GOC by Various agencies or their families. Monies are also used to educate the public about prevention of child abuse.

(Q).Who do I speak to, about having your organization visit and speak at my facility Church, Children's Home, PTA, etc...?
(A).You can contact The President of the Chapter in your area.

(Q).What if I want to start a chapter in my area?
(A).Contact the Chapter Development or the Ambassador on the National Page....www.guardiansofthechildren.com

www.guardiansofthechildren.com

We get a lot of people asking how they can help out or join GOC. We have a supporter level and a full patch member level. This week we will give a few bits of information on how to become a full patch member. (Reminder - GOC is an international non-profit organization with chapters all over the US and Canada.)

-It's best to start by attending a public monthly meeting. GOC has meetings every month.

-If you are interested in joining after learning more at the meeting, a background check and application are submitted through a designated board member.

-The background check costs $35.

-Once a background check is returned free from any abuse charges, the prospective member gains access to chapter communications, receives a road name, and is allowed to participate in adoptions and other GOC functions.

-The prospective member must attend all mandatory events (meetings, adoptions, child-related functions) for a period of time set forth by the chapter board. For most, this time period is a year.

-During the "probationary" period, the member is treated as any other, but does not wear the full back patch or have voting rights or rights to be a primary point of contact for a child.

-Once the member receives the full back patch, they are able to be a point of contact for a child and they have voting rights in the organization. They must maintain 70% participation in mandatory events.

-Patched members must own a motorcycle or have access to a seat on one (e.g., a husband may own a motorcycle and the wife rides with him.)

-Our primary mission is to "recognize and react to child abuse and educate the public to do the same," but being part of the organization usually means you become part of a big happy family. We all have each other's backs!

If you or someone you know may need our assistance, please go to www.guardiansofthechildren.com and from the Menu, locate the nearest Chapter to you. From that link you can email or call that Chapter to talk to someone.

RIO BRAVO PROJECT

Rio Bravo Project serves children in the border town of Juárez, Mexico. Through unique programs we provide children with positive choice to the dangerous alternatives found on the streets in their communities.
Each week we provide nearly 100 children with free jiu jitsu classes, literacy down dusty dirty streets, children arrive knowing they will find friendly faces that will love and and meals. Walking care for them. At each of our programs children are provided a meal prepared by a local family
that works with Rio Bravo Project. By providing a space for children to be children, we are able build relationships with them and their families in order to share God's love. You can find out more by visiting our website or following us on Facebook and Instagram.

If you have any questions please feel free to email our director
steve@riobravoproject.com

Website: riobravoproject
Facebook: facebook.com/riobravoproject
Instagram: instagram.com/riobravoproject

ACKNOWLEDGMENTS

We would like to extend a special thank you to these two fine ladies. They were instrumental in making this project real. Both were completely willing to jump into a new experience and help bring this to life. If ever you are in need of their services, please reach out.

Jennifer Kizziah

Born and raised in Lubbock, TX and schooled at Texas Tech University, I am a Red Raider through and through. I live out in the country with my husband, three kids and a menagerie of animals. When I'm not volunteering, some of my hobbies and passions include coffee, watching Tech basketball and anything Jane Austen. In early 2022 I started my own business, You & Stella, which is a personal and administrative assistant company providing services on a contract labor basis.
Contact information: jennifer@youandstella.com, www.youandstella.com

Michelle Burrus

Michelle Burrus is a middle school English teacher in Lubbock, Texas. She began her career teaching elementary school, and has just transitioned into the Educational Technology Director role for her district. She graduated with a Bachelor's degree in Early Childhood education from Lubbock Christian University. She enjoys spending time with her husband, three kids, and her dog, Tucker.
michellejburrus@gmail.com

www.ingramcontent.com/pod-product-compliance
Lightning Source LLC
Chambersburg PA
CBHW071956110526
44592CB00012B/1110